up down across

up down across

Elevators, Escalators, and Moving Sidewalks

Edited by Alisa Goetz

National Building Museum
Washington, D.C.

MERRELL
LONDON · NEW YORK

First published 2003 by Merrell Publishers Limited

Head office:
42 Southwark Street
London SE1 1UN
www.merrellpublishers.com

New York office:
49 West 24th Street
New York, NY 10010

in association with

National Building Museum
401 F Street NW
Washington, D.C. 20001
www.nbm.org

Published on the occasion of the exhibition
Up, Down, Across: Elevators, Escalators, and Moving Sidewalks
National Building Museum
September 12, 2003 – April 18, 2004
Curator: Abbott Miller
Assistant Curator: Alisa Goetz

This publication and the accompanying exhibition are sponsored by United Technologies Corporation and its subsidiary, Otis Elevator Company, that has moved people "up, down, across" for 150 years.

A catalogue record for this book is available from the Library of Congress

British Library Cataloguing-in-Publication data:
   Up, down, across : elevators, escalators and moving sidewalks
   1.Elevators 2.Escalators 3.Passenger conveyors
   4.Architecture, Modern
   I.Goetz, Alisa II.National Building Museum (U.S.)
   724.6

ISBN 1 85894 213 6 (hardcover edition)
ISBN 1 85894 214 4 (softcover edition)

Produced by Merrell Publishers Limited
Designed by Abbott Miller and Jeremy Hoffman, Pentagram Design, Inc.
Copy-edited by Lucinda Hawksley
Indexed by Diana LeCore

Printed and bound in Spain

Front and back jacket/cover: Escalators illuminated at night on the façade of the Georges Pompidou Center, Paris. Agnès Bichet/Photononstop

Pages 1 and 3: Details of an advertisement for Otis Elevator Company, 1952. Courtesy Otis Historical Archives

Contents

Elisha Otis demonstrating his safety brake at the Exhibition of the Industry of All Nations at the Crystal Palace, New York, 1854.

"All safe, gentleman, all safe," proclaimed Elisha Otis in 1854 after demonstrating his safety elevator at the Crystal Palace in New York City. The demonstration was simple: his assistant raised the platform on which Mr. Otis stood to a level well above the crowd's head, the traditional hemp support-rope was cut, and the platform fell but swiftly locked in place, proving the integrity of its mechanical safety device. The crowd roared, Elisha Otis's story quickly spread, and an industry was born.

This invention is captured as U.S. patent 31,128, "Improvements in Hoisting Apparatus." Often the most influential inventions are the most simple. Mr. Otis's safety elevator has reshaped urban landscapes and redefined the world's skylines.

We are pleased to sponsor *Up, Down, Across*, elucidating and enlivening elevators, escalators, and moving walks and, at the same time, celebrating the 150th anniversary of Otis Elevator Company.

George David
Chairman and Chief Executive Officer
United Technologies Corporation

Ari Bousbib
President
Otis Elevator Company

Foreword
Up, Down, Across:
Elevators, Escalators, and Moving Sidewalks

Howard Decker

View from the metro station of the National Building
Museum, Washington, D.C., formerly the Pension
Building, designed by Montgomery C. Meigs, 1887.

There is one type of transport in our urban centers that we all share no matter what we do to fill our days, where or how we live, or what we may prefer as our mode of travel: elevators, and their kin. Few technologies have exerted more force in shaping the American built environment, and this catalog, published in conjunction with an exhibition at the National Building Museum also entitled *Up, Down, Across: Elevators, Escalators, and Moving Sidewalks*, explores this shaping of our cities and towns from a variety of perspectives. Without the elevator, the skylines of America's cities, and cities all over the world, would be radically different: the canyons of any dense, noisy, and bustling metropolis would resemble prairies rather than the mountain ranges they have become.

Elevators, escalators, and moving sidewalks have become ubiquitous. Not only are they a functional necessity for most of our daily lives, guaranteeing basic mobility, but they pervade our social and cultural life as well. We have developed extensive social conventions as a way of dealing with them, from where to stare in a crowded elevator to where to stand on a crowded escalator. And these places have become an active part of our culture, whether in cinema, fiction, or other popular culture. This catalog illuminates these and other issues.

Generous support for the creation of this effort has come from United Technologies Corporation and the Otis Elevator Company, who this year

9

Looking skyward inside the atrium of the Hyatt Regency hotel, Atlanta, designed by John Portman, 1967.

celebrate the sesquicentennial of Elisha Otis's demonstration of the first "safety platform" at the 1853–54 Exhibition of the Industry of All Nations at the Crystal Palace in New York, thus permanently changing urban skylines the world over.

This catalog and exhibition arise from a collaborative effort by a dedicated team. Central to this effort has been the work of Assistant Curator Alisa Goetz, whose research forms the basis of this project and who conceived of the themes and elements of the work with David Gissen, former Curator of Architecture and Design for the National Building Museum and now an Assistant Professor of Architecture at Penn State University. Abbott Miller, of Pentagram Design, Inc., has acted with skill and imagination as the exhibition's guest curator and designer, and the catalog's designer as well. Museum volunteer Richard Evans has been of great assistance as he ably assisted Alisa in many months of research for the exhibition. Dr. Lee Gray, Associate Professor of Architecture at the University of North Carolina, Charlotte, acted as a content consultant, and Robert Vogel, Curator Emeritus of the Smithsonian Institution and one of America's leading historians of technology, acted as technical consultant. We also thank Robert Caporale and his staff at the industry publication *Elevator World* for all their help. And, finally, we thank our co-publishers at Merrell, and in particular Julian Honer, Merrell's extraordinary editorial director.

From the Eiffel Tower to elevators in outer space, the object of all our work has been to explore and celebrate a technology that has assured some of the greatest icons of the built world. Whether up, down, or across, we can be confident that architects and engineers will continue to move us as they transform the spaces in which we live, work, and play.

Howard Decker
Chief Curator
National Building Museum

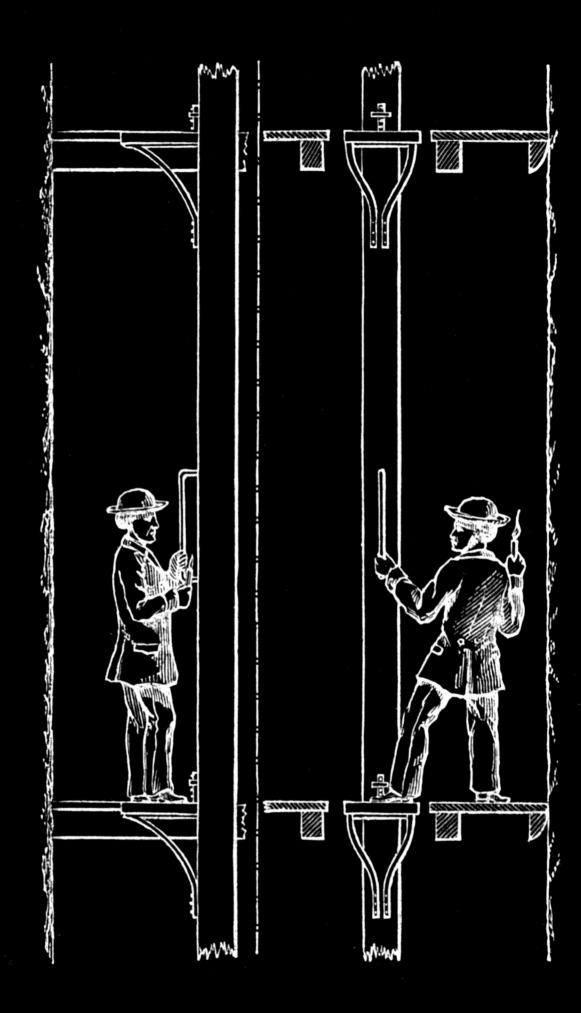

"Man engine," a mining elevator from the early nineteenth century. Some of the first people to use elevators in their daily work were miners. In Germany, England, France, lifts like the one depicted here were used nearly 200 years ago.

The courtyard of the Boreel Building, New York, 1881, showing hydraulic elevators. One of the first office buildings to have a bank of hydraulic passenger elevators was the Boreel Building in New York City. Between 1880 and 1900 nearly every building ten to twelve stories high featured hydraulic elevators.

Station on the movable sidewalk at the Exposition Universelle, Paris, 1900. The moving sidewalk at the Paris Exposition was the first practical application of the technology for touring. The *trottoir roulant*, as it was called in France, ran at an elevated height so that travelers could look down on the activities below.

Public lift and observation tower (the "Elevador de Santa Justa"), Lisbon, Portugal, 1901. One of the major impacts of the Eiffel Tower was that it allowed people to view the city as never before—from above. Since that time, the ability to look out over a vista has remained a major tourist draw, and influenced the construction of this pylon in Lisbon, which also connected two sections of the city.

A movable ramp at the Exposition Universelle, Paris, 1900. Though the first escalator was made publicly available for the entertainment of visitors to the Paris Exposition of 1900, movable ramps similar to the one pictured above had been used for amusement four years earlier. In 1896, inventor Jesse Reno installed an inclined "escalator" at Coney Island.

Apartment house lobby, 200 West 57th Street, New York, 1931. Though elevators in commercial use were fairly standard throughout the first half of the twentieth century, they were still seen as luxury items for residential use. The apartment buildings that could afford elevators tended to bathe their lobbies in elegance to show off this amenity as a status symbol.

Escalator in Redelsheimer's Department Store, Seattle, c. 1906. Besides providing a respite from the necessity of taking the stairs in department stores, escalators also created new patterns of shopping. Now that upper levels were as accessible as the first, products that people commonly purchased were separated on to different levels, forcing the customer to look through many additional products that might tempt them while hunting for their necessities.

Reno moving stairs on elevated lines, New York, *c.* 1900. With similar rapidity to department stores, systems of mass transit also picked up on the positive attributes of escalators. This particular escalator installation was one of the first after the Paris Exposition of 1900.

OPPOSITE **"Artist's Conception of New Modern Escalators," Union Pacific Station, Omaha, 1939.** Escalators quickly became standard equipment in many transit systems around the world. They were so popular, in fact, that an addition or update to a system often warranted its own advertisement.

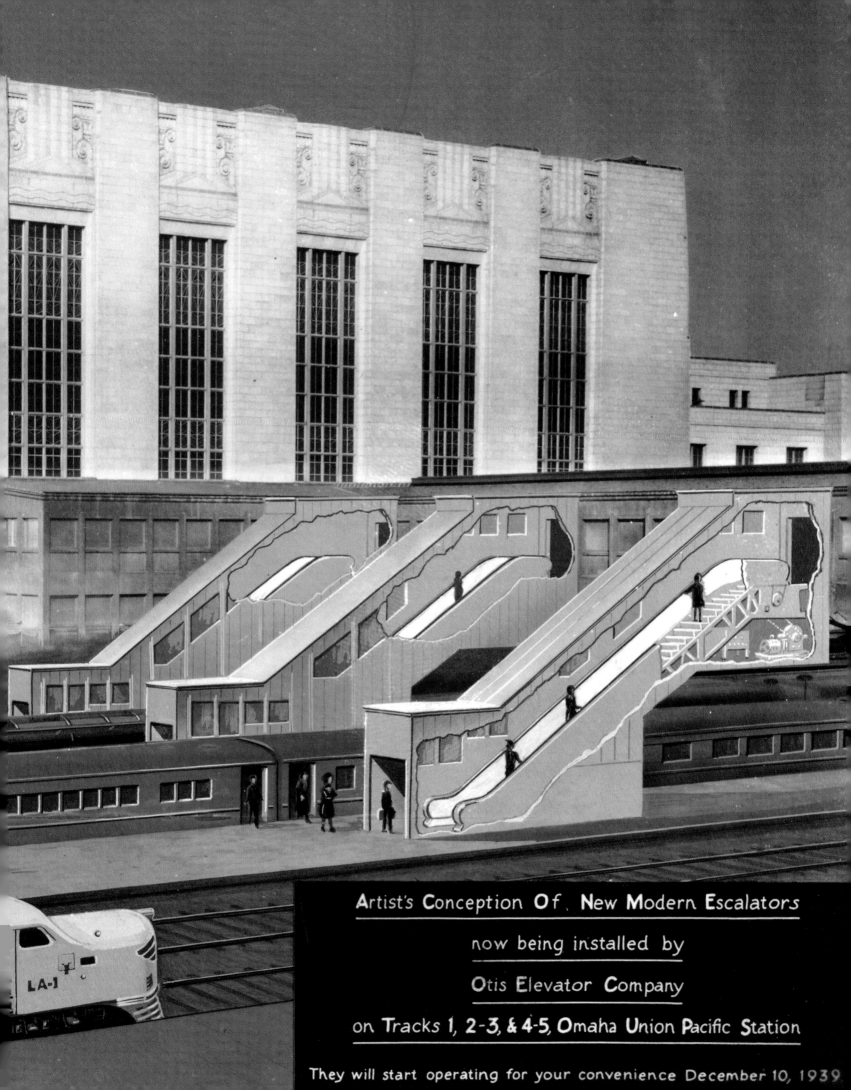

Artist's Conception Of New Modern Escalators

now being installed by

Otis Elevator Company

on Tracks 1, 2-3, & 4-5, Omaha Union Pacific Station

They will start operating for your convenience December 10, 1939

Escalators in Highgate Underground Station, London, 1931. Escalators were quickly embraced by most subway systems becuase they could constantly move commuters to and from stations. However, it took eleven years after the Paris Exposition for London Underground to install its first two escalators, in 1911.

LONDON
CO-OPERATIVE
SOCIETY L'TD

DO NOT SIT ON TH

Lobby of the United Nations Secretariat Building, New York, designed by Le Corbusier and Wallace K. Harrison, 1952. New construction and the modernization of elevators turned to stainless steel in the 1950s. The material provided a sleek, clean look that minimized the presence of the elevator, which was by then considered more of a utilitarian device than a luxury and opportunity for design.

Exterior elevator at the Town Hall, Mitte, Berlin, 1993. Prior to the elevator's widespread use in office and residential buildings, lower floors were considered more desirable because less stair-climbing was necessary. However, the incorporation of elevators made upper floors preferable as they were further removed from the noisy streets.

Exterior elevator at an office building (Lutz Bürogebäude), Berlin, 1994. In the 1970s, new developments in hydraulic technology brought down the expense of elevator installation. Since then, more and more low-rise buildings have either been designed with elevators or retrofitted to accommodate them.

Tram inside the St. Louis Arch, St. Louis, designed by Eero Saarinen, 1966. While it is mostly elevators that travel up monuments and towers to a panoramic view, the transport system in the St. Louis Arch is actually a combination of train, elevator, and amusement-park ride. The barrel-shaped cars rotate within individual frames so they are kept vertical while travelling the arch's incline.

Elevators in the Town Gate building, Düsseldorf, Germany, 2001. Since 1976, when the architects of the Pompidou Center in Paris pulled the escalator from the central interior of the building to the outside, new conceptions of conveyance design have become popular. In this example, the skeleton of the elevator system, though located inside the building's atrium, has been pulled out of the shaft and left visible to striking effect.

Reform Plaza, Warsaw, Poland, 1999. The panoramic or see-through elevator has been a great boon to retail and multi-use buildings. It shares the escalator's great advantage of allowing riders to see what they are passing, but also accommodates people who must use wheelchairs and strollers to get around.

Mixed use of conveyance devices at the Town Gate building, Düsseldorf, Germany, 2001. Many buildings now take advantage of the safety, effciency, and design potential of escalators and elevators by integrating both into their traffic patterns. The ten high-speed elevators and three escalators in this Düsseldorf building serve as highly visible design elements that introduce the theme of motion into the architecture while providing employees with quick navigation through the building.

Moving walkway, UnderWater World™, San Francisco, 1997. Moving sidewalks are particularly useful for moving crowds of people through large spaces at a steady rate. For that reason they have become popular with indoor attractions like UnderWater World™, where a glass-lined tunnel with a walkway offers visitors a diver's-eye view of the aquarium.

The Dungeon Drop ride at Six Flags Astroworld, Houston, Texas, 1997. Though elevators were made reliably safe for passengers 150 years ago, many people still fear being trapped in an elevator plunging uncontrollably to the bottom of the shaft. Popular culture has promoted this fear through movies, television, and even amusement park rides that offer the "thrill" of the free fall.

An elevator in a house in Bordeaux, France, designed by Rem Koolhass, 1998. Architect Rem Koolhaas designed this private residence in France for a wheelchair-bound client. Instead of using the standard installations that often look like an afterthought, Koolhaas made this elevator and its shaft the central core of the house, opening up the possibilities of design for special-needs clients.

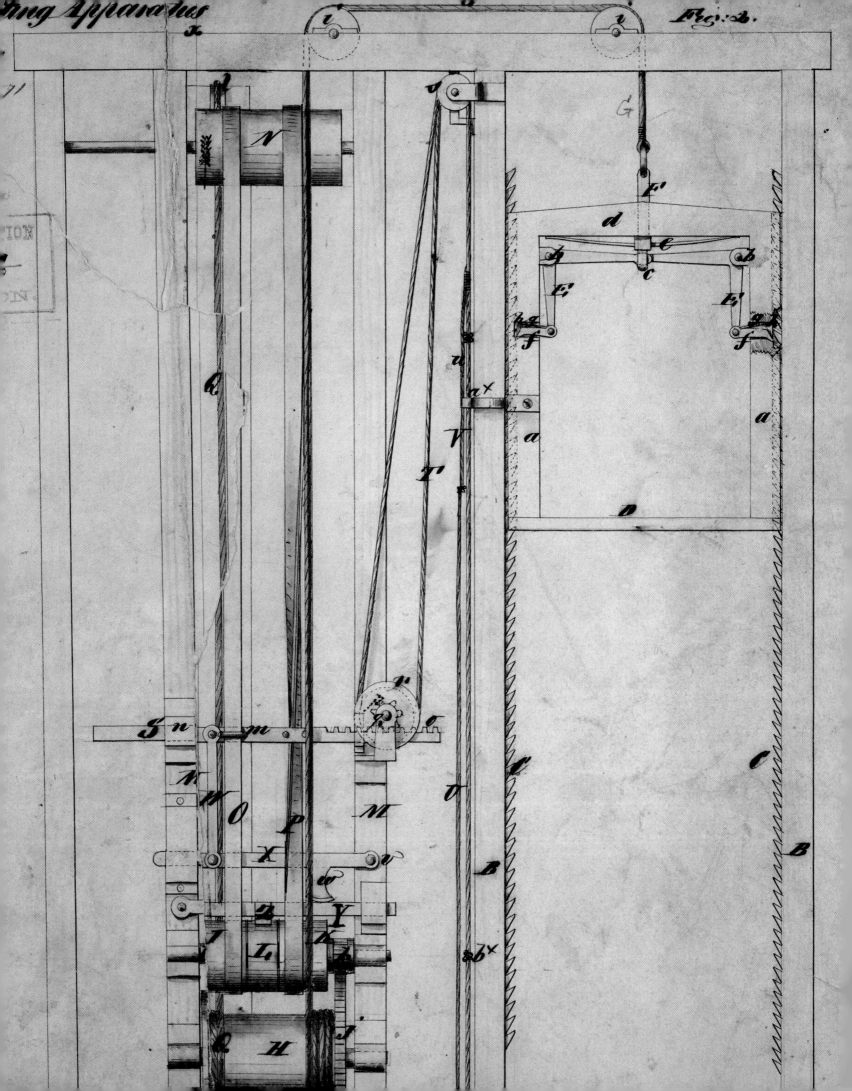

Vertical, Horizontal, Diagonal

Dr. Henry Petroski

001
Detail of a patent drawing for a safety brake for elevators, designed by Elisha Otis, 1861.

We live in a world of directions, with gravity defining the vertical, the distant horizon the horizontal, and deviations from them the diagonal. To get from point A to point B in the three-dimensional grids of technology that we call office buildings, airport terminals, department stores, and modern cities, we tend to be constrained to moving in rectilinear steps—up, down, left, right—and so we welcome opportunities to cut corners and travel along diagonals. We also accept gladly the mechanical assistance of an elevator, escalator, or moving sidewalk along the way.

The concept of a mechanical elevator is as old as the lever and the pulley, but passenger-carrying elevators as we know them date from the nineteenth century. People ceded space on early elevators to freight, because early elevators were prone to going into free fall when a lifting rope broke. It was the mechanical engineer Elisha Otis who invented a safety device that stopped a free-falling elevator in an instant. He showed its operation in a dramatic demonstration in the iron-and-glass Crystal Palace that was erected for the international exhibition held in New York City in 1853–54. As Otis stood in the open elevator car, high above a crowd of watching fairgoers, he cut the supporting rope, but the car dropped only a short distance before being stopped abruptly by a spring-loaded ratchet mechanism [001].

Otis Elevators

The achievement of this Company in perfecting the highest type of elevators has gained for its product recognition as the standard of excellence throughout the civilized world,—for

Quality, Safety, Efficiency, and Permanency

Otis Elevators are the ONE thing that has made possible the construction of the Titanic structures of stone and steel that everywhere today dot the marts of trade and industry,—the ONE thing that has heightened the "sky line,"—and marvelously increased the land values of the world's greatest cities, insuring to them unlimited development, concentration, and prosperity.

A particularly noteworthy example of recent contract is the battery of Otis Elevators being installed in the New Woolworth Building, Broadway and Park Place, New York,—the tallest building in the world, and the highest Elevators ever built—a rise of 51 stories from first-floor to dome—679 feet 6 inches.

This installation consists of the following groups:

Main Group—
Elevators—Nos. 1, 2, 23, 24,
    Otis Traction Machine.
Rise—1st to 51st Floor—679' 6''.

Main Group—
Elevators—Nos. 3, 22.
Rise—Basement to 40th Floor—530' 5½''.
    Otis Traction Machine.

Main Group—
Elevators—4, 5, 6, 7, 9, 10, 15, 16, 18, 19, 20, 21.
Rise—Basement to 27th Floor—358' 5½''.
    Otis Traction Machine.

Elevators—11, 12, 13 and 14.
Rise—1st to 12th Floor—144' 0''.
    Otis Traction Machine.

Elevators—8, 17.
Rise—S/B to 27th Floor—372' 11½''.
    Otis Traction Machine.

Combination Passenger and Freight Elevators.
Nos. 25 and 26.
Rise—Basement to 28th Floor—373' 5½''.
    Otis Traction Machine.

Passenger (Bank) Elevator—No. 31.
Rise—Basement to 4th Floor—56' 5½''.
    Otis Drum Type Machine.

Passenger (Tower Shuttle) Elevator—No. 34
Rise—51st to 54th Floor—47' 0''.
    Otis Drum Type Machine.

Ash Lift—Elevator No. 33.
Rise—S/B to S/W 29' 5½''.
    Otis Drum Type Machine.

We make Elevators of every type to meet every condition of freight and passenger service, including Inclined Freight types, and Otis Escalator or Moving Stairway. Otis Elevators should be used for modernizing old buildings, and for insuring the greatest convenience, economy, and satisfaction in the new.

Without obligation our Engineering Department will supply full information. Correspondence invited. Write to us.

Otis Elevator Company
17 Battery Place, New York

Offices in all principal cities in the world

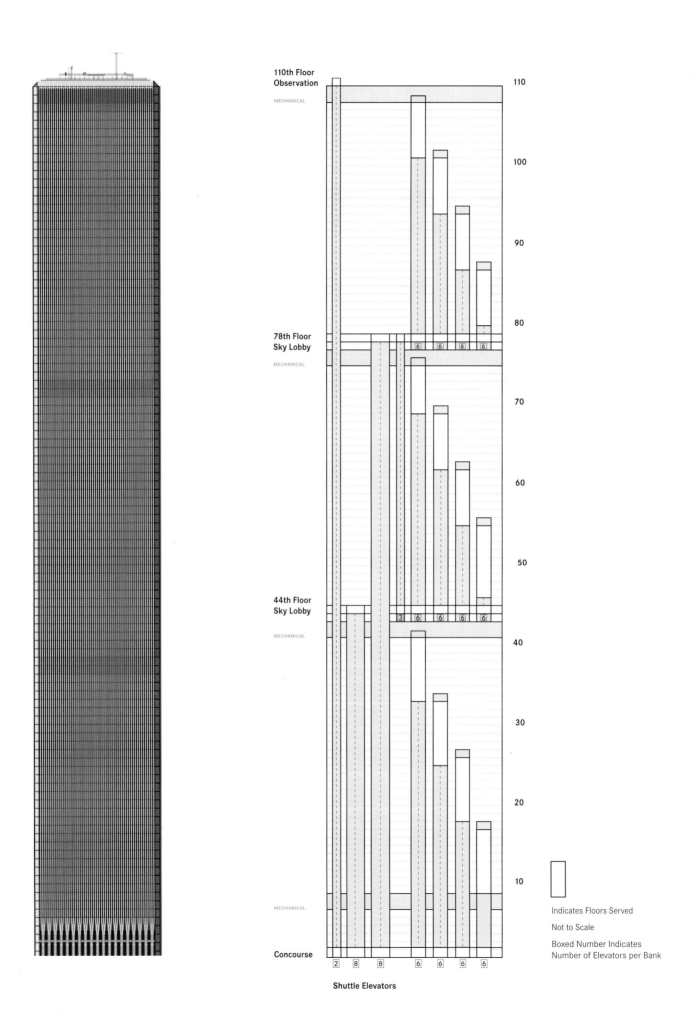

110th Floor
Observation

MECHANICAL

110

100

90

80

78th Floor
Sky Lobby

MECHANICAL

| 6 | 6 | 6 | 6 |

70

60

50

44th Floor
Sky Lobby

MECHANICAL

| 3 | 6 | 6 | 6 | 6 |

40

30

20

10

MECHANICAL

Concourse

| 2 | 8 | 8 | 6 | 6 | 6 | 6 |

Shuttle Elevators

Indicates Floors Served

Not to Scale

Boxed Number Indicates
Number of Elevators per Bank

With the fear of falling addressed, elevators soon began to be installed in high-rise buildings, which in the middle of the nineteenth century had meant five or so stories, a limit set by the number of flights of stairs that most people were willing to walk up to get to their apartment, office, or business. Elevators, of course, made taller buildings practical, and by the turn of the century, ten- and twelve-story skyscrapers were prominent, especially in cities like New York and Chicago. New York's twenty-one-story Flatiron Building, completed in 1902 and officially known as the Fuller Building, was famous for its hydraulic elevators [003]. The action of hydraulic cylinders on ropes and pulleys raised and lowered the elevator cars. A piston raised the elevator in its shaft, much as a hydraulic lift does an automobile in a garage. The principle underlying the operation of the Flatiron's elevators continued to be a topic of discussion among visitors to the building until their replacement in 1999.

Lifting an elevator car by cables from above made even taller buildings practical, and banks of elevators occupied prime space in the lobbies of structures such as the 1913 Woolworth Building (containing fifty-seven stories) and the 1930 Chrysler Building (seventy-seven stories), each of which was once the tallest in the world [002]. The elevators in these buildings were designed as ornate rooms with entrances consistent with their structure's respective Gothic and Art Deco architecture. The Chrysler Building, the first one-thousand-foot-tall skyscraper, held the height record for just a brief time, since the Empire State Building was completed the following year. At 1250 feet (380 meters) and 102 stories, the Empire State dwarfed everything in its neighborhood, and it still does. However, buildings over about seventy or eighty stories tall, while clearly structurally achievable, turned out to be economically inadvisable. Elevators, which made the skyscraper possible, now limited its height, and the Empire State remained the tallest building in the world for four decades.

The problem is not that elevators cannot be installed in the conventional way in office buildings much taller than the Empire State or the Sears Tower. It is that so many elevator shafts have to be built to accommodate all of the people expected to use them—the mostly empty shafts take up more valuable rental space than most investors are willing to cede to the structure and its vertical transportation system. Buildings as tall as 110 stories were not thought to be economically justified until the concept of a sky lobby was introduced in the early 1970s in the twin towers of the New York World Trade Center [005, 006]. In this scheme, express elevators transport passengers from the ground-floor lobby to transfer floors, where they move to local elevators. In this way, more than one elevator can use the same shaft, thus reducing the amount of space in the building taken up by elevators, and effectively providing more rentable office space. Another space-saving scheme is to have double-decker elevators, in which passengers use one or other of the levels depending upon whether their ultimate destination is an odd- or an even-numbered floor [004]. The use of multiple elevators to reach a high floor was once thought to be unacceptable to office workers and visitors, but the introduction of the scheme into the World Trade Center proved it to be effective both in saving space and moving people. Today, sky lobbies are not uncommon. Sadly, as was demonstrated during the World Trade Center disaster, sometimes more thought has been given to moving people under normal conditions than during emergencies, when elevators become disabled.

The word "elevator," in the sense of a device that raises or lifts something up, has its origins in the seventeenth century and thus predates its adaptation for the people-moving device. The word "escalator," on the other hand, was the creation of the Otis Elevator Company and, at first, it was not allowed as a descriptive term by the U.S. Patent Office. However, the neologism was registered

007 TOP
Exterior escalator at the Pompidou Center, Paris, designed by Richard Rogers and Renzo Piano, 1977.

008 ABOVE
The *trottoir roulant* (moving sidewalk) at the Exposition Universelle, Paris, 1900.

009 OPPOSITE
Escalators installed in the Gimbel Brothers Department Store, Pittsburgh, Pennsylvania, 1901.
From Frank Creden, ed., *Tell Me About Escalators*, Farmington CT (Otis Elevator Company) 1974.

as a trademark in 1900, which was the same year that the first escalator was put into public use at the Paris Exposition. After the fair, the moving stairway was disassembled and shipped to Philadelphia, where it was installed in the Gimbel Brothers Department Store [009]. The first escalator in London was also put into a department store, Harrods, in 1898. It was only during the Great Depression that the word "escalator" came to refer to upward or downward adjustment in wages or prices, and it was not until World War II that the word "escalate" was introduced to describe increasing military action.

Perhaps the most visible moving stairway in the world today is the cascade of escalators that are cantilevered out from the side of the Centre Georges Pompidou in Paris [007]. Enclosed in what appear to be glass tubes that snake up the side of the museum building, like a graph of ever-escalating prices, the stairway of escalators provides its riders with a breathtaking view of the city.

A ride on most escalators does not come with such striking views, of course, but it can provide a brief respite from the day's activities. Thus, a ride up an escalator is the setting for Nicholson Baker's novel *The Mezzanine* (1988), in which the device is the only way a worker can reach his office, since the elevators do not stop at the in-between-floors balcony level where it is located. Among the many mundane things the protagonist reflects upon during his ascent after lunch-hour is the way a maintenance man standing still beside the escalator polishes its entire handrail by just holding his cleaning rag against it while it moves like a conveyor belt past him.

Unlike an elevator, especially a high-speed one, which starts and stops with a noticeable jerk, the escalator can be mounted and dismounted with barely a loss of step. The clever morphing of the grooved stairs out of and into a solid floor enables us to move easily from one to the other. Seasoned travelers at airports can even roll a piece of carry-on luggage on to the step behind them without looking back. Because of escalators, the ride up to the ticket counter or down to the baggage claim area is as smooth as the take-off and landing of a jumbo jet.

Airports are also the most common venue for encountering the flat moving sidewalk or walkway, which (perhaps counter-intuitively) is a little trickier than the escalator to mount and dismount. Unlike the two-dimensional motion of the diagonal device, in which the well-practiced act of climbing stairs is simply given mechanical assistance, getting on to a moving sidewalk can feel like a rug is being pulled out from under one's feet. Disembarking can be like ice-skating off a frozen pond and on to a dry concrete walk. It is no wonder that the approach to the end of a moving sidewalk is often heralded by flashing lights and repetitive recorded warnings.

The moving walkway is not a jet-age invention, however. A "moving pavement," which may be thought of as a flat escalator, was installed at the same Paris Exposition that introduced the escalator [008]. The elaborate installation involved three parallel "sidewalks," one of which was fixed, the second of which moved at about normal walking speed, and the third of which traveled at twice that rate. Unlike today's moving sidewalks, which we step on to head-on, those in Paris in 1900 were mounted from the side, with the middle walkway providing a transition from the slow to the fast lane. Using a moving walkway is actually not a very difficult thing to do for people accustomed to jumping on or off an open streetcar or cable car—or accustomed to getting on and off a ski lift or a constantly moving amusement ride like the Millennium Wheel now installed beside the River Thames in London.

Like the introduction of anything new into society, that of elevators, escalators, and moving sidewalks necessitated the evolution and promulgation of rules of etiquette associated with their use. Hence the unspoken rule, at least in America, of facing forward in elevators, and on escalators and moving walkways

Elevator cores under construction in 1993 at the Luxor Hotel and Casino, Las Vegas, designed by Klai Juba and Veldon Simpson.

of standing on the right and passing on the left. Cultural differences between countries in which driving is done on different sides of the road can lead to awkwardness, confusion, and frustration in using mechanical people movers in cosmopolitan settings, such as large cities and international airports.

The more familiar we become with anything, whether mechanical or not, the more we expect a certain predictable behavior from it and so adjust our own behavior accordingly. Thus, we learn to absorb the forces associated with the starting and stopping of conventional elevators by flexing our knees to the appropriate degree. When elevators travel in an unconventional direction, as they do up the inclined legs of the Eiffel Tower or along the edges of the pyramid-shaped Luxor Hotel in Las Vegas, their starting and stopping can throw us off balance sideways, as if we were standing on a bus that made an unexpected turn. The experience is especially disorienting in the Luxor, where there is no visual clue in the windowless elevator car, which otherwise looks like an ordinary one and gives no hint that it will move in any way but vertically [010].

People are enormously adaptable, however, and in no more time than it takes newly arrived Luxor guests to leave their luggage in their room and change into their gaming clothes, they learn to brace themselves sideways in the elevator car that takes them down to the casino. In just as quick a fashion, we also learn to mount escalators with nary a misstep, though most of us will never quite adjust to the handrail that slips and so moves slower than the moving stairs themselves. All things mechanical have their quirks and their personalities, just like the people who use them, and sometimes they work better than at other times. We all have our up days, our down days, and our diagonal days.

Dr. Henry Petroski
A.S. Vesic Professor of Civil Engineering
Duke University, Durham, NC

1

Turning Point:
Conveyance and the
Paris Exposition of 1900

Alisa Goetz

A moving sidewalk panorama, Paris, 1900. From
Marius Bar and José de Olivares, *The Parisian Dream
City*, St. Louis (N.D. Thompson Publishing Co.) 1900.

**"The machine has taken over control of the entire world. It is replacing
workers, employing them in its service and expanding the relations
between the peoples of the earth."** Alexandre Millerand, Paris Exposition
of 1900[1]

The theme of the Exposition Universelle et Internationale de Paris, 1900, was
"A Century in Retrospect," but when Trade Minister Millerand made the above
statement, he was referring to the overwhelming presence of technology at the
Exposition, not the art, armor, and colonized peoples that were also on display.
The year 1900 and the Exposition marked a turning point for technology. People
were beginning to understand how electricity worked and what potential it held
for the future. Though the phenomenon of electricity had been exhibited at the
1889 Paris Fair, it was referred to as "a fairy of the nineteenth century,"[2] and considered magic rather than scientific discovery. By 1900, electricity was not just
an attraction in itself, but garnered interest as a method of providing light, power,
and movement [023]. Industrialists, fair officials, and visitors alike had an early
look into how electricity would transform industries such as transportation.

For the first time, millions of people were able to experience mechanized vertical, diagonal, and horizontal movement all in one place. Although the elevator

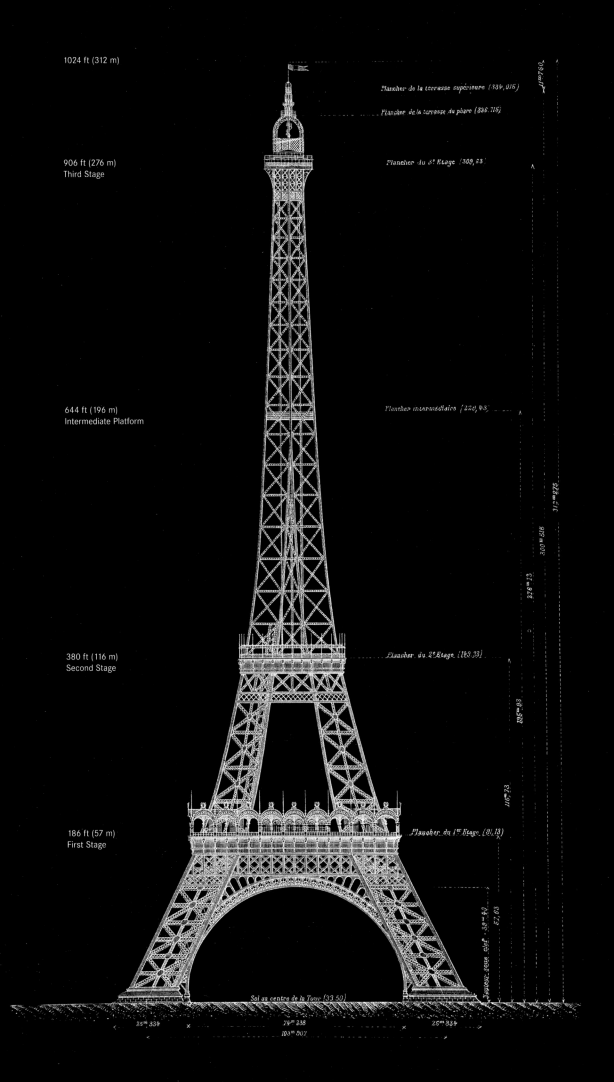

1024 ft (312 m)

906 ft (276 m)
Third Stage

644 ft (196 m)
Intermediate Platform

380 ft (116 m)
Second Stage

186 ft (57 m)
First Stage

Plancher de la terrasse supérieure (334,015)

Plancher de la terrasse du phare (336,715)

Plancher du 3e Etage (309,63)

Plancher intermédiaire (228,43)

Plancher du 2e Etage (149,23)

Plancher du 1er Etage (91,13)

Sol au centre de la Tour (33,50)

1m760

312m275

300m515

276m13

195m93

116m73

Hauteur sous clef 58m40

57,63

25m334   74m238   25m334

103m307

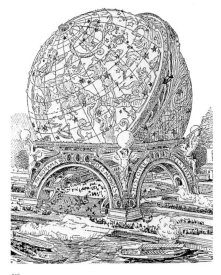

012

The Celestial Globe at the Paris Exposition Universelle, 1900. From Barrett Eastman and Frédéric Mayer, *Paris, 1900: The American Guide to City and Exposition*, New York (Baldwin & Eastman) 1899.

013   TOP

The machine and cabin designed by Roux, Combaluzier, and Lepape for the Eiffel Tower, Paris, 1889.

014   ABOVE

Passengers changing cars on the Edoux Elevator at the intermediate platform in the Eiffel Tower, Paris, 1889. From *La Nature*, May 4, 1889.

015   OPPOSITE

Stage diagram of the Eiffel Tower, Paris, designed by Gustave Eiffel, 1889. Adapted from Gustave Eiffel, *La Tour de Trois Cents Mètres*, Paris, 1900.

had been around for some time, the addition of electricity made it faster and more efficient, while it made the escalator and moving sidewalk at the 1900 Exposition popular amusements.

Yet, nearly fifty years earlier, the elevator had made an even more spectacular display. At the New York exposition of 1853–54, Elisha Otis had demonstrated his invention—the elevator safety brake—in dramatic fashion. He stood on the raised platform of his elevator and cut the rope supporting it. Much to the crowd's amazement, the elevator did not fall. It was the most significant innovation for the elevator to date, and ushered in a new era in which passenger elevators would change the architecture of cities.

By the time of the 1900 Paris Exposition, elevators had been integrated into several buildings and attractions for reasons of practicality and entertainment. The U.S. Pavilion housed two elevators servicing four level; the Subterranean Mining Exhibition used regular mine elevators to give the impression that visitors were actually being lowered into the ground; and the Celestial Globe utilized electric elevators to convey fairgoers into an interior sphere representing the center of the planetary system [012]. The Eiffel Tower, however, erected at the 1889 fair, still drew large crowds from among the fifty-one million people in attendance.[3]

When it was built, the Eiffel Tower stood 986 feet (300 meters) tall and contained five hydraulic elevators by three different manufacturers [015]. At that time, electric elevators were considered technically too risky for this difficult construction.[4] Double-deck elevators by the French company Roux, Combaluzier, and Lepape ran in the east and west piers from the ground to the first platform [013]. Otis elevators lifted riders from the ground and first platforms to the second platform in the north and south piers [017]. The third elevator system, made by Leon Edoux, a leading French elevator manufacturer, combined two elevators and a transfer platform at an intermediate level to send passengers to the uppermost platform [014].[5] It took seven minutes to travel from the ground to the top of the Eiffel Tower, and 455 people per hour could make the trip.

The tower was such a popular attraction, able to turn a profit within its first year, that for the 1900 Exposition officials decided to transform and replace the existing elevators to accommodate larger crowds. The Otis elevator in the north pier was preserved, but altered to carry eighty passengers per trip instead of the forty-two it originally held. The other Otis was removed from the south pier and replaced by a wide stairway that ran from the ground to the second platform. The elevators in the east and west piers gave way to completely new hydraulic systems by the Compagnie de Fives-Lille.[6] It is interesting to note that people were, and still are, very willing to pay the fees associated with visiting the different levels of the Eiffel Tower. For many, the bird's-eye view of Paris was the first they had ever experienced, and certainly worth the wait and cost [016]. Standing on the top platform provided a view of 80 miles (130 kilometers) in every direction on a clear day.

The Eiffel Tower offered a new view of the world, and it was only possible because of elevators, but the escalator, also at the 1900 Exposition, offered a method of transportation that was entirely new. What seems so commonplace to us now, was then an amusement that riders paid for the privilege of experiencing.

The earliest escalator-like machines had been patented in 1892, but those were fairly different from what is referred to as an "escalator" today. Jesse Reno designed and patented what he called the "endless conveyor or elevator" [018]. That same year, yet independently, George Wheeler invented and patented a flat-step "inclined elevator" [020]. Though the 1900 Exposition identified the creations as "movable ramps," both inventors used the term "elevator" to

A

B

C

Exposition Univ... — Tour Eiffel, Promenoir du 1er Étage. ND. Phot.

126

016 ABOVE
**The promenade of the first level of the Eiffel Tower,
1889.** From *The Eiffel Tower: A Tour de Force, Its
Centennial Exhibition*, exhib. cat., ed. Phillip Dennis Cate,
New York, The Grolier Club, 1989.

The first platform of the Eiffel Tower was not only
popular for the view but also for the four restaurants
with varying prices to accommodate the wide variety
of visitors.

017 OPPOSITE
**Details of the construction of the Eiffel Tower
elevators by Otis Elevator Company, 1889.**

G. A. WHEELER.

ELEVATOR.

No. 479,864.

Patented Aug. 2, 1892.

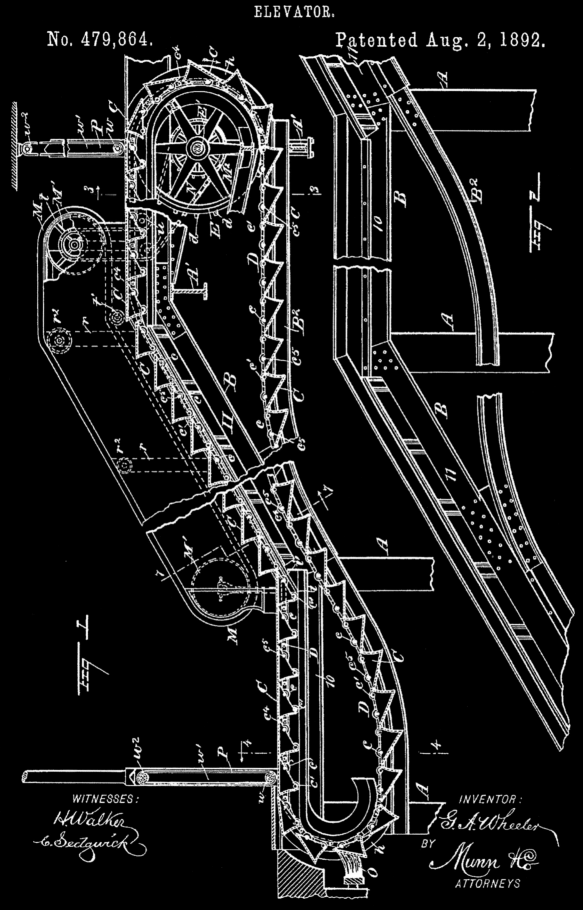

WITNESSES:

H. Walker

C. Sedgwick

INVENTOR:

G. A. Wheeler

BY

Munn & Co.

ATTORNEYS

describe their devices. At that time, the word "elevator" was being used in a broad way to refer to any machine that moved people upward.

An issue of *Scientific American* from 1900 discussed all the movable ramps at the Paris Exposition—there were thirty-one of them. It also singles out the Otis Escalator that "consists of a true stairway which moves in a lump."[7] Though the mention is brief, this escalator was to have a major impact, becoming the standard used in department stores, shopping malls, transportation stations, and office buildings alike. The Otis Elevator Company, with the help of Charles Seeberger, who had taken over Wheeler's patents, designed the Paris Escalator, which had the risers and treads of an ordinary staircase and kept the steps where riders entered and exited level with the surrounding surface [019].[8]

During the course of the Exposition, the idea of an escalator gained widespread popularity in Paris when one became a feature in the Palace of Thread, Fabrics, and Clothing. This escalator promoted the idea of "shopping" while "riding." Since it was not an enclosed space like the elevator, and a rider only had to stand still, his or her attention could be turned toward the surrounding products and displays. This idea was furthered when the very escalator introduced at the Paris Exposition was subsequently transferred to the Gimbel Brothers Department Store in Philadelphia.

In the U.S., other uses for the escalator were also being discovered. The recent installation of a so-called Reno Inclined Elevator at an elevated station in Manhattan signaled the desire for an efficient way to move large groups of people up to the trains [021]. The escalator's easy embarking and disembarking points made it a practical success and have led to its installation throughout most subway systems to this day.

The elevators, movable ramps, and the escalator were not the only methods for moving people around the Paris Exposition. One more conveyance device, which had made its popular debut at the World's Columbian Exposition of 1893 in Chicago, was the movable elevated platform or moving sidewalk. For the Chicago Fair the movable sidewalk traveled 4300 feet (1300 meters) along a pier and contained seats that held up to four people [022]. Curiously, it was still referred to as a sidewalk even though passengers were meant to sit while riding.

The moving sidewalk at the Paris Exposition traveled a much greater distance than its predecessor had, seven years earlier, and had a more useful purpose. The platform was a little longer than two-and-a-half miles (four kilometers), taking the form of an irregular quadrilateral that moved passengers among different sections of the Exposition [025]. It was made up of three tracks, the first being stationary, and the other two moving at half and full speed in order to ease the transition from stillness to movement. Next to the stationary track ran the half-speed track at approximately two-and-a-half miles (four kilometers) per hour. The full-speed track ran next to the half-speed track at five-and-a-quarter miles (nine kilometers) per hour [024].[9] Each ride, regardless of distance, cost 10 cents. The attraction ran from morning to night and offered glimpses into the residential life of the city as well as attractions at the Exposition.

On average, 160,000 passengers per day used the moving sidewalk. It had two main purposes: as a method of touring the Parisian landscape, and as a form of transportation among the different areas of the Paris Exposition. The platform was elevated to the second level of the Exposition's buildings and gave riders a view of all the happenings within the Exposition's grounds as well as of the finest roofs in Paris. Residents whose homes were passed by the walkway complained about the noise and lack of privacy, but no amount of complaints was going to stop the moving sidewalk from running.

As a vehicle for travel around the area, the moving sidewalk had one major advantage over the electric railway (which ran close by): the sidewalk allowed

018 TOP
Patent drawing of the "endless conveyor or elevator," 1892. From George R Strakosch, ed., *The Vertical Transportation Handbook*, 3rd edn New York (John Wiley & Sons, Inc.) 1998.

019 ABOVE
Longitudinal section through the stairway shown at the Paris Exposition, 1900. From *Scientific American*, November 17, 1900.

020 OPPOSITE
Patent drawing of George Wheeler's flat-step elevator, 1892.

Escalator employed by the Interborough Rapid Transit Co. at 23rd St. & 6th Ave., New York, 1903.

The movable sidewalk at the World's Columbian Exposition, Chicago, 1893. From James W. Shepp and Daniel B. Shepp, *Shepp's World's Fair Photographed*, Chicago (Globe Bible Publishing Co.) 1893.

riders to enjoy the weather and the sights and the sounds of the Exposition without being enclosed inside a rail car [011]. In the evening, riders could enjoy a spectacular view of the various pavilions and attractions decked out in thousands of differently colored electric lights.

Much like the escalator, the moving sidewalk was also a method of conveyance that required no waiting. A steady stream of riders could mount and dismount the sidewalk at their own pace, eliminating the need to crowd on to a platform waiting for a train to arrive. Though the sidewalk was popular at the Paris Exposition, it never achieved the widespread success of the elevator or escalator. One reason may be simply that railway cars can move at a much higher speed, making them more effective for commuting. Additionally, the moving sidewalk leaves the rider exposed to the elements. For Paris in the summer this was a benefit, for commuters in New York in the winter it would not be.

Moving walkways have found their niche, however. They can be seen on a visit to almost any large airport anywhere in the world, moving travelers among gates, counters, and concourses. They have also recently become popular again for touring and amusement purposes. Several aquariums, museums, and theme parks use the sidewalks to glide people through attractions and exhibitions. At San Francisco's Pier 39, UnderWater World™ turns the aquarium inside out by having visitors glide through a transparent tube on a moving walkway as the surrounding marine life passes by. Disneyland in California also uses moving walkways in a practical way. They are transitional devices between the standing line and the ride vehicles, as in The Haunted Mansion. In this attraction, the moving sidewalks help visitors into and out of their "Doom Buggies," which do not have to stop to load and unload passengers.

Paris during the 1900 Exposition offered a wealth of attractions and experiences to the turn-of-the-century visitor, but perhaps none was more extraordinary than the variety of methods of transportation available, especially when coupled with the use of electricity for practical and reliable power. The visitors who went up, down, and across were some of the first to use conveyance devices that, as Alexandre Millerand predicted at the beginning of the Exposition, would change the world.

For *Up, Down, Across: Elevators, Escalators, and Moving Sidewalks*, six insightful essayists analyze the ways in which these conveyance devices have changed and continue to change the world. From how we get to work, to where we live, to what we do in our spare time, elevators, escalators, and moving sidewalks have all had a hand in transforming our everyday lives.

When the passenger elevator became a reliable means of moving people through multi-story buildings, the questions of its operation and interior appearance became issues. Early on, the skills of the elevator operator gave way to impersonal automatic control panels that hid the complexities of elevator control. Elevators were converted from elegant rooms to mere confined spaces to potentially visceral experiences, where anything is possible. Author Peter Hall discusses how the elevator car has been transformed in presentation and design, though not in basic function.

Escalators and moving sidewalks have also undergone an evolution of sorts. Their adaptability to a variety of uses has been a catalyst for moving faster, making elegant curves, and providing a diversion to weary passengers. Not only have the machines themselves changed, but also our perception of them. Author John King explains why people in the U.S. tend to take escalators and moving sidewalks for granted, while people nearly everywhere else are taking advantage of the spectacular views and design possibilities they offer.

ÉCOLE
MILITAIRE

AVENUE DE LA MOTTE PICQUET

NATIONAL
MANU-
FACTURES.

DIVERSIFIED INDUSTRIES

HOTEL
DES INVALIDES

AGRICULTURE

HALL
OF
FESTIVALS

AG

MACHINERY

ELECTRICITY

Chateau d'Eau

ESPLANADE DES INVALIDES

DECORATION
AND FURNITURE

BOULEVARD DE LA TOUR MAUBOURG

LA BOURDONNAIS

TEXTILE
INDUSTRIES

CHAMP
DE
MARS

DES INVALIDES

AVENUE BOSQUET

TEXTILE
INDUSTRIES

4

5

8

6

7

9

VILLE DE PARIS

PAVILIONS OF

10

11

12

AVENUE RAPP

AVENUE

MINES
AND
METALS

26

13

14

15

16

17

18

19

20

21

22

23

24

HORTICULTURE AND ARBORICULTURE

PASSERELLE FOREIGN NATIONS

SOCIAL ECONOMY CONGRESSES

32

29

30

28

31

27

ADMINISTRATION

25

Pont de L'Alma

ARMY AND NAVY

MERCHANT
MARINE

MONTAIGNE

PLACE
DE
L'ALMA

OLD PARIS

PASSERELLE

AVENUE DE L'ALMA

PLEASURE BOATS

42

64

AVENUE MARCEAU

AVENUE DU

O' IÉNA

TROCADÉRO

Place d Iéna

66

67

65

FOREIGN

62

61

61

60

6

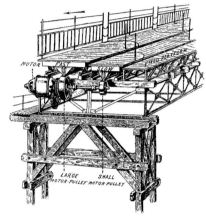

023 TOP
The Palace of Electricity at the Paris Exposition Universelle, 1900.

The Palace of Electricity featured an electric fountain with water that flowed over multicolored lights. The spectacle it made at night was so breathtaking that it was referred to as "a vision of fairy splendor."

024 ABOVE
Mechanism of the rolling platform, 1900. From *Scientific American Supplement*, no. 1279, July 7, 1900.

025 OPPOSITE
Map of the grounds at the Universal Exposition, Paris, 1900. From *The Pocket Guide to the Universal Exposition, Paris*, New York (W.R. Jenkins) and London (Baillière, Tindall & Cox) 1900.

This detail of the map shows the route of the moving sidewalk, an irregular quadrilateral in shape.

Though technical innovations from the 1850s to the present have led to a worldwide explosion in the number of elevators, it tends to be their design that attracts newsworthy attention. One of the best-known architects of buildings with show-stopping elevators is architect John Portman. First gaining popularity with his Hyatt Regency Hotel in Atlanta during the 1960s, Portman went on to design the Bonaventure Hotel in Los Angeles and the Renaissance Center in Detroit. In an interview with the architect conducted specifically for this book, author Phil Patton explores the elevators of John Portman and their forerunners.

In author Keller Easterling's essay about fully automated buildings, design takes a backseat to function. Since the 1939 New York World's Fair, the dream of omni-directional automated conveyance has interested engineers and urban planners alike. Though not yet realized on Interstate Highways, these systems have been adopted by the shipping and warehousing industries. Large tracts of land from Hong Kong to Rotterdam to Texas have become sites where fully automated warehouses can operate almost without human interaction—a logician's dream come true.

The pervasiveness of elevators, escalators, and moving sidewalks in today's society has been explored from the perspective of mechanics and design, but perhaps it can best be appreciated through the lens of art. After all, it has been said that art imitates life. Through postcards, advertisements, and paintings we have developed a certain level of comfort with the escalator as a transportation device. Author Julie Wosk analyzes what the presence of the escalator in photography and art says about our culture.

Broadening the scope of art to motion pictures, literature, and Internet presentations, author Susan Garfinkel presents the elevator as a vehicle for thought-provoking interaction. Through art, elevators take on their own persona, and become metaphors for change, often from an orderly status quo to some chaotic state. They also play a part as the location of discovery, suspense, and emotionally driven actions.

Each essayist examines elevators, escalators, and moving sidewalks from a different angle. Design, function, and representation are addressed as discreet aspects, creating a more complete vision of the impact of conveyance devices on our world today.

1. Opening speech at the Paris Exposition of 1900 by Alexandre Millerand, Socialist Minister of Trade, April 14, 1900.

2. Commissioner General of the 1900 Paris Exposition, Alfred Picard, referred to electricity in this way. See Theodore Stanton, "The International Exhibition of 1900," *The Century Magazine*, vol. 51, no. 2, 1895, p. 316.

3. Arthur Chandler, "Culmination: The Paris Exposition Universelle of 1900," *World's Fair* magazine, vol. 7, no. 3, 1987, revised 2000.

4. Robert M. Vogel, *Elevator Systems of the Eiffel Tower 1889*, Washington, D.C. (Smithsonian Institution) 1961, p. 14.

5. Joseph Harriss, *The Tallest Tower: Eiffel and the Belle Epoque*, Washington, D.C. (Regnery Gateway) 1989.

6. *La Nature*, "The New Elevators of the Eiffel Tower," *Scientific American Supplement*, no. 1301, December 8, 1900, pp. 20851–52.

7. *La Nature*, "Movable Ramps at the Paris Exposition," *Scientific American Supplement*, no. 1297, November 10, 1900, p. 20790.

8. *Scientific American*, no. 83, November 17, 1900, p. 313.

9. "The Rolling Platform at the Exposition of 1900," *Scientific American Supplement*, no. 1279, July 7, 1900, pp. 20504–05.

2

Designing Non-Space:
The Evolution of the Elevator Interior

Peter A. Hall

Elevator with wood-finish interior, mid-twentieth century.

"Arbo equipped their newest model with an oversized door to foster the illusion of space, to distract the passenger from what every passenger feels acutely about elevators. That they ride in a box on a rope in a pit. That they are in the void." Colson Whitehead, *The Intuitionist* [1]

The idea that, in entering an elevator, we are entering a kind of limbo, a transitory space where gravity is momentarily defied, lurks behind the entire history of the elevator interior's development. More than any decorative embellishments or surface treatments, awe and fear have defined the space since its invention. In *Delirious New York* (1978), Rem Koolhaas characterized the elevator as an invention loaded with contradiction: it "contained in its success is the specter of its possible failure." [2] For the elevator to gain public acceptance and cohabit with the skyscraper to alter city skylines irrevocably, Elisha Otis first had to perform a miracle at the New York Crystal Palace exposition of 1853–54. He cut the cable that had hoisted him above the assembled crowd. It snapped, the platform jolted, but Otis did not crash to the floor; his spring-and-ratchet safety brake had held him steady. "Thus Otis introduces an invention in urban theatricality," noted Koolhaas: "the anticlimax as denouement."

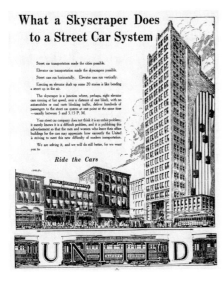

What a Skyscraper Does
to a Street Car System

Ride the Cars

UNITED

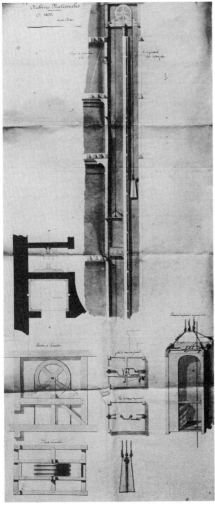

027 TOP
Advertisement for United Railways and Electric Company, Baltimore, 1927. From Paul Wirtz, ed., *Baltimore and Streetcars 1926*, Baltimore (Baltimore Streetcar Museum Inc.) 1988.

028 ABOVE
Drawing of a *chaise volante* (flying chair) for the Palace of Versailles, France, c. 1750. From Jean Gavois, *Going Up: An Informal History of the Elevator from the Pyramids to the Present*, Hartford (Otis Elevator Company) 1983.

029 OPPOSITE
Main elevator at the Hôtel Meurice, Paris, designed by Henri Nenot, 1907.

The elevator interior is a space that is strikingly difficult to fit into a design discipline. Does it properly belong in the field of interior design, being a room that, by the way, just happens to move? Or should it fall under the jurisdiction of the transportation designer, since it is, in truth, a vehicle? Its early development is closely aligned with that of the streetcar, which in the late nineteenth century provided the appropriate crossover technology with electric motors to directly power the hoist [027]. Early elevators were even fitted with seats, so passengers could enjoy the ride [029]. The modern elevator, however, is unique in its spartan furnishing, odd psychological ambience, and limited control. It is difficult to think of another vehicle that we ride or operate without being able to see where we are going.

This wasn't always the case. Today's standard blind steel cabs belie the magical grandeur and thrill inherent in the invention at its conception. Reports of Louis XV's "flying chair" suggest a manual contraption of weights and pulleys attached to a seat. It was built at the king's palace in France in 1743 and used to hoist the royal occupant from the first to the second floor *outside* the building [028]. Early elevators, likewise, had little interior to speak of. To maximize the drama and visibility of the spectacle at New York's Crystal Palace, Otis was raised aloft on a platform without walls. The invention became a staple of the nineteenth-century world's fair, providing riders with a new perspective—a bird's-eye view of the terrain below. At the Jubilee Exhibition in Liverpool, England, in 1866, passengers were carried in a steam-powered lift to an observation tower, and by 1889, four water-pressure-powered hydraulic elevators (built by Otis and the French firm Roux, Combaluzier, and Lepape) were hauling passengers to the first and second stages of the Eiffel Tower. The tower, as Roland Barthes has written, was built for no particular purpose other than to be seen, and as a place from which to see. Its elevators, slow-moving boxes with windows on all sides, reminiscent of hot-air balloon baskets, became, like the tower, both spectacle and vantagepoint.

Nineteenth-century engineers were not just demonstrating the steam and hydraulic-powered defiance of gravity; they were striving to bring humankind closer to God. David Noble argues in *The Religion of Technology* (1997) that Victorian engineering drew much of its robust spirit from religious thought dating back to the Carolingian age, which first began to cast man's artificial contrivances as a means of redemption.[3] By the eighteenth century, the approach of the new millennium was fueling fervent speculation of a "mechanized return to Eden," writes Noble, and by the late nineteenth century, the engineering mission was clearly defined. James Clerk Maxwell, whose electromagnetic equations of 1873 set down the theoretical basis for the development of the electric motor (which in turn came to drive the evolution of the elevator), wrote daily prayers for guidance in harnessing technology "that we may subdue the earth for our use." The American engineer and steam-power specialist Robert Thurston predicted in *Science* magazine that man should be able, by perfecting energy utilization, to reach a sort of technologically assisted enlightenment: "He may profit," wrote Thurston, "by all opportunities of advancing himself to loftier and loftier planes, perfecting himself."[4]

The elevator made loftier planes literally accessible, providing riders with God-like, panoramic views of His creation, a view that, according to Barthes, allowed people to "transcend sensation." Two million people ascended the Eiffel Tower in its first year of opening.

The open design of the first elevators persisted through the first half of the twentieth century, notably in the lifts still found in luxury European hotels and apartment buildings where the ornate metalwork of a gilded cage is often positioned at the center of a spiral staircase—an arrangement with cinematic

61

LOCAL TO 11TH FLOOR

030 **The Hudson Terminal Building, New York, designed by Clinton & Russell, 1896.**

031 OPPOSITE **Elevator in a residential building, Berlin, 1910.** From Kerstin and Alfred Englert, *Lifts in Berlin*, Berlin (Jovis) 1998.

034
Elevator attendant, *c.* 1900, Zurich, Switzerland.

potential exploited in many mid-century movies featuring chase-the-elevator-down-the-stairs scenes [031]. But the need for riders to be able to see out during their ascent inevitably lost ground to commercial considerations as demand grew for cost-effective vertical transportation in the residential high-rises rapidly proliferating in densely populated cities. By the late 1890s, New York City could boast more than 5000 apartment elevators. The window onto the world began to diminish to the point where it would become little more than a grille-covered peephole in the door for establishing the cab's arrival.

Enclosure turned the rider's attention inward, robbing him or her of a sense of direction and accentuating the mystery of vertical transportation. Lacking a suitable model for designing this briefly inhabited moving space, architects and their clients, including those owning luxury apartment buildings, began to obliterate all evidence of its transient function. Late-nineteenth-century elevators had included seats, for enjoying the slow climb, but by the 1920s, in Manhattan's wealthier buildings, elevator cabs were becoming intricately decorated rooms, furnished to match the grandeur and permanence of the buildings. The architecture firm Warren and Wetmore's 1929 design for an apartment building at 230 Park Avenue, for instance, featured red-walled elevators with domed ceilings bedecked with painted clouds, miniature chandeliers, and plaster moldings. William Van Alen's Chrysler Building of 1930 offered curved car interiors inlaid with fleur-de-lis motifs of teak, mahogany, walnut, prima vera, maple, ebony, and oak—sourced from around the world [033].

One astute observer of the dream-like anachronisms inherent in such baroque cladding of state-of-the-art technology was the Surrealist Salvador Dalí. Riding an elevator in a Manhattan apartment building in 1935, he noted: "I was surprised by the fact that instead of electricity it was lighted by a large candle. On the wall of the elevator there was a copy of a painting by El Greco hung from heavily ornamented Spanish red velvet strips."

In *Delirious New York*, Koolhaas casts this episode as part of Dalí's antimodern "discovery" of New York, a revelation that supports Koolhaas's reading of the city as an outrageous outcrop of the Machine Age, or a "costume ball" of Modern architecture. Van Alen, he notes, attended a Beaux-Arts costume ball dressed in a cape made of "Flexwood" modeled on his elevator doors. Koolhaas also comments: "Only in New York has architecture become the design of costumes that do not reveal the true nature of repetitive interiors, but slip smoothly into the subconscious to perform their roles as symbols."

At the core of this citywide building beauty contest, in which exteriors flamboyantly refused to reflect interior function and vice versa, the elevator cab became a kind of inner sanctum of illusion, distilling the disconnection between mechanism and form with metaphorical hocus pocus. With the small wrought-metal grilles often included in the doors, the opulent box took on the character of a confession booth, recalling, perhaps, the spiritual aspirations of its Victorian inventors [030]. When the grille was dispensed with, the box became a magician's trick, a room that deposited its occupants in a different space—a room that changed the rooms outside. The resulting confusion for occupants is portrayed by Peter Sellers as the *idiot savant* Chauncey Gardener in Hal Ashby's 1979 film *Being There*.[5] On entering a heavily decorated elevator, Sellers's character remarks, "How long do we stay here?" On exiting, he exclaims, "That is a very small room."

When elevator manufacturers began to cut the human operator out of the equation, the void began to loom larger. Automation began as early as 1892, when apartment buildings in which a full-time attendant was deemed too expensive were equipped with push-button control [032]. Unlike today's push-button elevators, the nineteenth-century version could handle only one call at a time

65

and travel at speeds below 100 feet (30.5 meters) per minute. The fastest elevators now climb at 2500 feet (762 meters) per minute. In early automated elevators, a passenger entering the car would be taken to his or her destination without any stops; for those awaiting the car on other floors, this meant a waiting period that increasingly came to define the elevator experience.

The contrast between staffed space and empty, automatic space cannot be overemphasized. In the elevator's formative years, its interior was something of a performance space for its operators, who enjoyed a sixty-year starring role on the urban stage before machines could even begin to replace them fully [034]. Novels, cartoons, and films portrayed the operator as a quirky, sometimes belligerent character whose persona defined the mood of the car space. Such was the operator's prominence in daily life that one leaflet published by Otis in 1949 on "elevator etiquette" advised that long conversations with the operator should be avoided, as they "may result in missing stops."

The theater had other players too. At the turn of the century, as buildings rose in size and increased in capacity, they often required an entire staff to take charge of the logistics of choreographing ridership peaks. The eight new electronic elevators installed in the forty-nine-story Tower Building of the Singer Sewing Machine complex in 1906–08, for instance, were coordinated by an attendant positioned at a "starter's panel" on the ground floor [037]. This consisted of eight rows of miniature lamps, each row representing an elevator with a lamp for each floor of the building. The starter would keep track of the elevator's position according to which lamps were illuminated, and call directions to the in-car operators via a remotely operated directional light inside the elevator—or simply by shouting through a megaphone. This comic audio-visual signaling system was used in several major buildings until 1924, when the Standard Oil building in New York pioneered an electro-mechanical method of signal control, which partially replaced the starter.

The gradual replacement of operations staff with a push-button interface paralleled the ongoing drive toward automation in several industries. Even photography was being reduced from an elaborate ballet involving sliding glass plates and black-cloth hoods to a one-step process. With the Brownie camera of 1901, George Eastman captured the essence of effortlessness: "You press the button, we do the rest."

Pushing buttons similarly distanced the elevator rider from the raw mechanics of the ride. Early elevators had often been summoned by an attendant tugging on a "shipper rope" [035]. By the late 1920s, push-buttons and multi-voltage control (which eliminated sudden speed changes) were conspiring to insulate passengers from the tangible aspects of vertical travel, the shudders, the starters' shouts, and the operator's distinctive way of calling floors: "Mezzie" (mezzanine), "Lazy" (lobby), and so on.

Shortly after World War Two, the Machine Age dream of complete automation was nearing its climax. America had arrived at the "push-button age"—irons and washing machines were automatic, and advertisers and editors were conjuring up utopian scenarios in which the touch of a button would take care of all household chores, summoning not servants but "mechanical brides." Even automobile makers flirted with push-button control, advertising effortless gear-changing that suggested, forebodingly, the day of the driverless car [036].

Since machines have always elicited awe and fear of human obsolescence in equal parts, drivers hung on to the wheel and the sense of control they enjoyed from motoring, and some residents (as well as unions) clung to their beloved elevator operators. As late as January 1975, *The New York Times* was reporting a battle between residents of an East 66th Street apartment and their landlord, who had decided to automate the elevator and dismiss three operators.[6] Residents

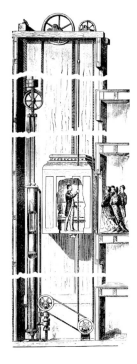

035 TOP
Operator controlling a hydraulic elevator by rope, c. 1881.

The attendant operated this hydraulic elevator by pulling on the rope that runs through the cab. This would open or close the valves that controlled ascent and descent.

036 ABOVE
Otis Elevator Company advertisement for signal control, first half of the twentieth century.

037 OPPOSITE
Hallway of the Singer Building, 49 Broadway, New York, designed Ernest Flagg, 1908.

claimed that their dismissal would jeopardize building security. It may also have jeopardized maintenance; a report later that year claimed that a national study had found breakdowns more likely to occur in operator-less elevators.

But the utopian connotations of rider-operated, push-button travel were hard to resist, seductively parceled up in the concurrent vision of futuristic cities of convenience, with skyscrapers and aerial gardens accessed by criss-crossing tiers of vertical transportation. As Thomas Hine has noted, push-buttons were sold as the "harbingers of a glittering, effortless future." The elevator's unique orientation promised equally effortless travel, perhaps eventually to outer space (an idea recently revived by the engineer of the World Trade Center, Leslie Robertson) or to the center of the earth. For the most part, the public bought into the myth. Otis's "Autotronic" control system, introduced in 1948 in buildings in Dallas, New York, Philadelphia, and San Francisco, was within just eight years being installed in every new commercial building contracted to the company [039]. Its silent choreography was no small leap from the raucous theater of the human-conducted Singer Tower Building. Computing power developed during the war provided an analog relay-based system based on Boolean algebra to count the number of rider calls registered on buttons in cars and halls, then add up the waiting time, establish car positions, and compile the information to dispatch appropriate elevators. Printed circuit boards eventually replaced the electro-mechanical system, controlling the high-speed elevators of the World Trade Center when it opened in 1973. It took fifty-eight seconds for passengers to reach the 107th floor. "It made me feel as if I were being transported to a different world," reminisced one passenger, William Grimes, in a tribute to what was for some time America's fastest elevator.

The ironic result of increasingly efficient vehicles was to make riders more impatient. Removing the driver took away the last possibility of palpable human error. Otis president Ralph Weller noted in 1953 that "much time is lost by slow-moving passengers who make no effort to hurry. They know the attendant will wait for them . . . but the impersonal operatorless elevator starts closing the door after permitting you a reasonable time to enter or leave." But the very same technological advance left riders with no outlet for their impatience and frustrations. The cheery or grumpy operator had been replaced with a faceless array of numbered disks that gave no indication that the rider's floor request had been registered [038]. Eventually, the cold cathode gas-filled tube, combined with an electronic circuit, provided the technology for the first buttons to light up when pushed.

Interface design has become an increasingly important preoccupation for designers—as artificial intelligence is increasingly incorporated into the built environment—but surprisingly little attention has been paid to the elevator interface. The easily confused "door open" and "door close" triangle symbols illustrate the apparent lack of attention paid to the issue. Door operation is automated, and more instinctively overridden, by activating the infra-red sensors or rubber safety shoes that prevent a door from closing on a passenger. Thus "door open" and "door close" have little function in the modern elevator other than for riders to mimic deftly the old-school chivalry or belligerence, respectively, of the human operator. Getting them mixed up raises the possibility of hapless employees closing the elevator doors on their colleagues, visitors, or bosses. According to the author James Gleick, many building managers choose to disable the "door close" button altogether.

Car call response is a source of frustration partly because passengers cannot see what is happening behind the shaft doors. Gleick reports that people begin to get "upset" after just forty seconds. Ground floor indicator panels—reminiscent of the earlier starter's panel—and floor-level directional arrows that light up

provide minimal information to waiting riders. But at the core of passenger frustration is the possibility that car coordination, along with the rest of the activity in the pit, is too complex—or mystifying—to comprehend. The interface problem continues to prompt an array of explanations and quick-fix solutions. An Otis-commissioned report of 1979, cited by Gleick, postulates that the anxiety of the waiting rider looking upward reflects a primal fear of attack by "airborne predators." Gleick maintains that it is our increasing appetite for speed that makes the wait seem interminable. An apocryphal tale surrounding the Westinghouse engineer George C. Sziklai, who was responsible for the high-speed elevators installed in Mies van der Rohe's 1958 Seagram building, suggests that riders can be easily pacified with the help of vanity. After hearing complaints that the elevators were too slow, Sziklai installed a wall-to-wall mirror opposite the elevator bank to distract waiting passengers. The complaints ceased immediately [043].

Reflective surfaces, in fact, have long provided a solution to the rush of claustrophobia felt by riders entering the tiny cabs. "Walls and ceilings of stainless steel or mirrored bronze can make cars look larger," advised one contractor in a *New York Times* report of 1992.[7] "Women can primp. I myself straighten my tie" [040]. Yet mirrors also reflect rider behavior back to them, reiterating their plight. Psychologist Andrew Baum was quoted in the *Times* story suggesting that, since the amount of personal space in a cab is "inadequate," the elevator presents a "violation of intimacy." But even in a spacious car, rider behavior becomes conspicuous. The silenced, enclosed cab has the effect of exaggerating every rider noise, move, and gesture. Indeed, the potential for erotic liaisons with friends or strangers in elevator cars, coupled with the possible thrill of sudden exhibitionism, has become a movie trope in itself as a result of these peculiar acoustic and social conditions [041].

Forced intimacy may fuel rider discomfort (or erotic fantasies), but a deeper anxiety amplifies the experience—fear of entrapment, or death. The subject has been endlessly popularized by the news and film media, enchanted with its theatrical potential. There is a Walt Disney World ride, "Tower of Terror," that simulates a series of drops in a creaking 1939 Hollywood hotel elevator. News indexes routinely list tales of children falling into shafts, crushed limbs, falling elevators, and office workers trapped over weekends. Cab design after the war did little to dilute the macabre associations. Low-cost residential and office high-rises were equipped with standardized elevators, which generally took one of two design routes: the reflecting effect of stainless steel, or the fake wood veneer, a descendant of the car-as-moving-room concept [026]. The author Colson Whitehead does not hesitate to venture the grim implications of design treatments in his dark novel *The Intuitionist* (1999), which concerns the adventures of a mid-century elevator inspector:

"There's an old inspector's maxim: 'An elevator is a grave.' Such loss and devastation in there. That's why the inside walls of the car are never sheer; they're broken up into panels, equipped with a dorsal rail. Otherwise it would be a box, a coffin."

The darkest reality of the low-cost residential elevator is not its morbid ambience, however, but its social context. Urbanist Jane Jacobs took a moment in *The Death and Life of Great American Cities* (1961) to point out the hazards of the elevator-serviced apartment building, the most efficient and, under unfavorable circumstances, most dangerous way of packing people on a given amount of land: "The corridors of the usual high-rise, low-income housing buildings are like corridors in a bad dream: creepily lit, narrow, smelly, blind. They feel like traps, and they are. So are the elevators that lead to them."[8]

Jacobs's bad dream permeates even the cocaine-fogged mind of jazz trumpeter Miles Davis in a particularly downbeat moment of his autobiography.

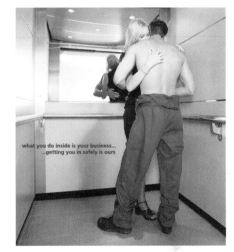

041 TOP
Advertisement for the elevator safety company T.L. Jones Microscan, *c.* **2002.**

042 ABOVE
A Captivate television in an elevator, *c.* **2002.**

043 OPPOSITE
Mirrored elevator car interior, 2000.

Mirrors in elevators remain a popular design strategy today.

In a fit of paranoia, he runs from his car to a building elevator: ". . . a woman was on the elevator. I thought that I was still in my Ferrari, so I told her, 'Bitch, what are you doing in my goddam car!' And then I slapped her and ran out of the building."[9]

Efforts to present an antidote to the post-war city-apartment "coffin" are found only, of course, on the opposite end of the social spectrum: the luxury hotel and high-end office building. The best-known efforts are curiously ephemeral. Muzak, or elevator music, invented in the 1920s by General George Squier to calm "nervous riders of a new gadget called the elevator" in department stores, these days replaces deafening silence (rather than unnerving creaks) with saccharine sound. A more recent innovation is news and advertising broadcasted to flat-panel television screens installed inside the cab [042]. According to Captivate Network, a company founded in 1997 to target "affluent professionals," their TVs can be found in more than 7000 elevators across North America.

The elevator's architectural salvation, however, arrived in 1967 when the architect-developer John Portman completed the Hyatt Regency Hotel in Atlanta, with its pioneering set of "rocket ship" glass elevators. Over 10,000 people turned out to view the new $18-million hotel with its glass capsules rising up the side of a twenty-one-story atrium [045]. Statuesque tour guides dressed in silver space suits provided riders with a guide to the hotel's features, while lines of people in the courtyard below struggled to convince security guards that they too had room keys and should be allowed to ride the elevators.

The parallel between Portman's capsules and the first passenger elevators of the nineteenth century is striking. Glass elevators not only provided bird's-eye views for riders; from below, they also became what Portman called a "giant kinetic sculpture." Like Elisha Otis, whose safety device was simply a practical solution to a problem posed by an acquaintance, Portman had "backed into" the idea: having put an atrium at the center of the hotel, in a cramped area of downtown Atlanta, he chose to reduce service space by eliminating the shaft, pulling the elevators "out of the wall."

To capitalize on those tourists expected to come to the hotel only to ride the glass capsules, Portman put a revolving restaurant at the top of the building, above the atrium. Ascending riders literally went through the ceiling into the restaurant, where a dome provided panoramic views of the city skyline [044]. Portman's rationale was typically customer-"experience"-driven, and fully cognizant of the open elevators of edifices past. "We're all familiar with the old cage elevators of European hotels," he said, "but our idea was to take it even further, and make the trip from the registration desk to the room one of great interest." After the hotel's opening, Portman noticed an unexpected by-product: the passengers, unlike usual elevator riders, continued talking when they entered the cab. Portman's conclusion, that the design could affect rider behavior, is articulated in metaphysical, almost Victorian terms, "If you get in a closed-box elevator your spirit seems to be driven inward. People stand there or look at their feet. In a glass elevator, the spirit goes out and people continue their conversations."

The glass elevator has since become a common feature of hotels, retail malls, and luxury venues, where it is deemed desirable to encourage visitors to linger. Unlike the caged cabs of the elevator's golden years, glass offers the potential of complete, unimpeded visibility of Otis's original ascending platform, but with the security of enclosure. In Germany, where glass has become the definitive material of reunification and open democracy, the glass elevator is the embodiment of the idealized workings of government. In the Paul Löbe Haus parliament building adjacent to the Reichstag, transparency extends through to the service core, where fully glazed hoistways encase the movement of sixteen glass cars

044 ABOVE
The Polaris rooftop restaurant at the Hyatt Regency, Atlanta, designed by John Portman, 1967.

045 OPPOSITE
Elevated view of the atrium, Hyatt Regency, Atlanta, 1967.

046 TOP
Elevator core in the Paul-Löbe Haus, Parliamentary Committee Chambers, Berlin, designed by Stephan Braunfels Architects, 2001.

047, 048 ABOVE AND OPPOSITE
Elevators in the Paul-Löbe Haus, Parliamentary Committee Chambers, Berlin, 2001.

with illuminated floors and tilting ceilings [046]. The glazed shafts are, in fact, suspended from the roof of the building, enabling architect Stephan Braunfels to minimize the steel sections and convey the illusion of weightlessness. High visibility has proven particularly popular with journalists, since the elevators back on to the rotunda chambers where parliamentary sessions are held. "If there is an issue of public interest being debated, you see reporters gathering around the glass shafts to catch a glimpse," said Berthold Pesch, an architect at Stephan Braunfels. "The design stresses a kind of transparency in the political process" [048].

Transparency also serves to alleviate the anxiety of waiting passengers. "The technical staff from the Parliament wanted us to install displays on the floors to show what each elevator is doing, but as architects, we wanted as few displays as possible," says Braunfels. "We pointed out that you can see if something is moving or not by looking up the shafts" [047].

Dematerializing the interior comes at a price, however: the glass elevator is not a particularly cost-effective proposition. For example, the Paul Löbe Haus, as the seat of government, was expected to demonstrate high standards and therefore enjoyed a budget of $271 million, of which $7 million was spent on the elevators. Transparency seems, for the time being, to be destined to remain aligned with mercantile motives and elaborate political gestures. At the chic Chambers Hotel in New York's SoHo, elevator cab walls are glazed in a kind of artistic parody of the Portman idea. Located in their original position inside a conventional shaftway, the elevator walls simply provide a view of the inner workings of the building: concrete, metal girders, cables, and piping.

The history of elevator interior design might be summarized as a series of schizophrenic attempts alternately to celebrate and to disguise the awe and terror of vertical ascent, the miracle of levitation. In the fairground setting of the nineteenth-century exhibition grounds, the twentieth-century hotel and the twenty-first-century parliament building, the elevator interior vanishes, becoming a sublime spectacle and exalted vantagepoint [049]. In the enclosed environs of the building core, be it the surreal mobile room of the apartment building, or the perfunctory pistons of low-cost housing or corporate headquarters, the elevator interior becomes an attempt to disguise the mechanical activity and obscure computational logistics of pumping populations through the structures of work and rest. The gradual elimination of humans from the machine's operation has only added to its mystery and confirmed our suspicions that someone else, not present inside the car, is really in control, be it artificial intelligence or a supernatural or corporate entity.

The most vivid extrapolation of the elevator's tangled psycho-spatial themes is to be found, inevitably, in fiction. In the eerie near-future Tokyo cityscape of Haruki Murakami's novel *Hard-Boiled Wonderland and the End of the World* (1985; translated 1987), the elevator's portrayal as soulless, empty, automated piston finds its logical outcome as a polished steel interior stripped of all rider controls, from "close door" to emergency stop.[10] All power is conferred to the invisible corporate entity that owns the building. The large, hermetically sealed vault of a space, "antiseptic as a brand-new coffin," is so advanced that the narrator's coughs are dampened to a "dull thud" and all sensation of vehicular motion is absent. The result is complete spatial and temporal disorientation:

"The elevator continued its impossibly slow ascent. Or at least I imagined it was ascent. There was no telling for sure: it was so slow that all sense of direction simply vanished. It could have been going down for all I knew, or maybe it wasn't moving at all. But let's just assume it was going up. Merely a guess. Maybe I'd gone up twelve stories, then down three. Maybe I'd circled the globe. How would I know?"

049

Ostbahnhof train station, Berlin, refurbished in the 1990s.

But the more uplifting, aspirational alternative, the ascendant glass capsule, finds its apogee in Roald Dahl's children's book *Charlie and the Great Glass Elevator* (1972).[11] Here the transparent conveyance transports its occupants past their destination, a chocolate factory, and into outer space. Operated, somewhat unpredictably, by the mysterious Willy Wonka, the elevator–spaceship careens into view of a capsule of astronauts and U.S. space agency observers on earth, and snubs conventional science by beating the astronauts to a newly built, uninhabited Space Hotel. Wonka's method of navigating the ionosphere has a mystical flavor hinting at catharsis—or euphoria of the chemically induced variety: "We must go up before we can come down! We must go higher and higher!"

The vehicle is operated, naturally, with a panel of color-coded buttons.

"He pressed a brown button. The Elevator shuddered and then with a fearful whooshing noise it shot vertically upward like a rocket."

1. Colson Whitehead, *The Intuitionist*, New York (Anchor Books) 1999.

2. Rem Koolhaas. *Delirious New York: A Retroactive Manifesto for Manhattan*, New York (Oxford University Press) 1978.

3. David Noble, *The Religion of Technology: The Divinity of Man and the Spirit of Invention*, New York (A.A. Knopf) 1997.

4. Robert Thurston, *Science*.

5. *Being There*, director Hal Ashby, writer Jerzy Kosinski, 1979, Lorimar/North Star/CIP.

6. *The New York Times*, January 1975.

7. *The New York Times*, 1992.

8. Jane Jacobs, *The Death and Life of Great American Cities*, New York (Random House) 1961.

9. Miles Davis with Quincy Trope, *Miles*, New York (Simon & Schuster) *c*. 1989.

10. Haruki Murakami, *Hard-Boiled Wonderland and the End of the World* [1985], trans. Alfred Birnbaum, London (Hamish Hamilton) 1987.

11. Roald Dahl, *Charlie and the Great Glass Elevator*, New York (Knopf) 1972; reissued New York (Puffin) 1998, pp. 3–4.

Stand on the right

No smoking

A Matter of Perception: Escalators, Moving Sidewalks, and the Motion of Society

John King

Escalator at Angel Underground Station, London, 1995.

In the movie *Ordinary People* (1980), there's a scene where the upscale sub-urban mother, played by Mary Tyler Moore, drifts through the ether of Chicago's Water Tower Place. She floats upwards past cosmetics and clothing, detached, even when called to by a friend sliding down a few yards away. Pleasantries are exchanged, but neither person can pause. The moment pulls them apart.

The brief scene is about urban distance, how you can be isolated from the world though cloaked in all its affluent sensations. And the scene is about something else—escalators. Yes, escalators: how they shape our world, not just physically, but emotionally. They let you be a voyeur or be lost in your thoughts; either way, the journey's the same. The bare minimum of effort is enough to be transported, not stopping until you reach your preordained destination. It's a risk-free, out-of-body experience. Not even a button to push!

True, such notions might seem absurd for something so ostensibly mundane: escalators and their horizontal cousins, moving sidewalks, are the transportation equivalent of air-conditioning, the background hum of urban life. They shave a few seconds off the race to the subway, or make it easier to get from the security checkpoint to gate 57 [051]. The upper floors of department stores or malls wouldn't be nearly so beguiling without a stair-studded conveyor belt.

Yet, like air-conditioning, escalators and moving sidewalks are at the core of modern society—especially in central cities, where land is at a premium and the sky beckons. For, if elevators allow us to *scrape* the sky, escalators fill in the spaces between, where you want activity, bustle—not just the quiet of an office cubicle or a penthouse suite. They allow street life to expand like an accordion, up and down at once. They allow movement without exertion. At the very least, it's hard to imagine Mary Tyler Moore all brittle *ennui* if she'd just trekked up five flights of stairs.

The influence of what Jesse W. Reno patented in 1892 as "a new and useful endless conveyor or elevator"[1] is confirmed by no less a cultural arbiter than Rem Koolhaas and his Project on the City at Harvard University. The *Harvard Design School Guide to Shopping* (2002) devotes a thirty-page chapter to the invention, stating its case in absolute terms: "No invention has had the importance for and impact on shopping as the escalator," the chapter begins. "As an instrument of smoothness, the escalator triggered a vast new domain of construction, which—through the very smoothness of connection—we now inhabit almost without thought, and without any sense of its true scale or radicality."[2]

On a more subtle level (there's nothing subtle about Koolhaasian bombast) the impact of escalators is even more profound. Whether or not by conscious design, what they do is to frame our perception of a place. Anyone entranced by London can testify to this: when a newcomer slowly chug-chug-chugs up from the bowels of one of the older Tube stations, through a narrow tunnel lined with "adverts" for new movies and ale, the arrival at the surface mixes exhilaration with relief [050]. It's like some passage through time, a steep journey from London's past to the here and now. That final walk up to the street, and you have *arrived.*

There's a similar situation in Paris. Not at the Pompidou Center, though the glazed escalators that rise above Place Beaubourg are so popular that a recent renovation not only makes gawkers pay for the ride but also adds escalators *inside* to make life easier for exhibit-goers [053].[3] No, the memorable sensation comes right off the bat, in the international terminal at Charles de Gaulle Airport. First-time visitors arrive with eager dreams of history, the Sacré-Coeur, and the Louvre, so they're likely to be caught off-guard by zigzagging tubes suspended in air that provide a crash course on French culture's fascination with all things modern [054]. Sure, this brand of modernism dates back to the 1960s and could use some fine-tuning, but the gesture is as brash as ever. "It reminds me of *Space 1999*, a sci-fi series produced in the late 1970s," gushes a University of Houston student in an online campus paper. "The see-through tunnels covering the escalators going in all different directions gave an out-of-this-world feeling, which earned many whistles and cheers from the newly arrived American tourists, complete with mild curse words, all intended to communicate their approval."[4]

But you don't need to travel abroad to gain this effect. The lasting perception can be as simple as a view, a life-sized postcard if you will. The impression left by the vista at an escalator's summit is a message about the city around it. San Francisco shows this well: one escalator emerging from the subway below Market Street lines up directly with the Flood Building , a classic example of 1904 civic pride in a neo-Baroque vein, sandstone cloaked in giant columns and stiff cornices [056]. Another focuses on 595 Market Street, thirty-one stories of flat concrete and horizontal glass from 1979 [055]. The buildings couldn't be more different, yet each perspective sends the same message to commuters: this ain't the suburbs, pal.

After a ruinous 1972 earthquake, Nicaragua did without escalators for twenty-six years. Then two shopping malls opened in the capital city of Managua—each sporting endless conveyors—to decidedly mixed reviews [052]. In the early

051   TOP
Moving walkway at Buffalo Niagara International Airport, East Concourse Extension, Buffalo, New York, designed by Cannon Design, 2000.

052   ABOVE
Escalators at Metrocentro Managua, Managua, Nicaragua, c. 1998.

053   OPPOSITE
Riding the escalators at the Pompidou Center, Paris, designed by Richard Rogers and Renzo Piano, 1977.

055 **595 Market Street viewed from a Bay Area Rapid Transit Station escalator, San Francisco.**

056 OPPOSITE **The Flood Building viewed from a Bay Area Rapid Transit Station escalator, San Francisco.**

057 TOP
A moving staircase dividend warrant, Harrod's Stores Ltd., London, 1899.

058 ABOVE
Escalator at Leicester Square Underground Station, London, 1935.

059 OPPOSITE
Spiral escalator at Westfield Shoppingtown, San Francisco, 1988.

060
The escalator flat-step design by Charles Seeberger, c. 1900.

weeks at one of the malls, attendants dressed as storybook characters gave directions to nervous passengers. "Thrill-seeking kids crowd around the landings . . . daring one another to bolt down the rising stairs," a reporter noted, while a fifty-nine-year-old housekeeper demanded "What's going to keep me from being sucked into the ground down at the bottom of this thing?" Later she confessed to riding escalators in pre-earthquake days, "but I'm not as young as I used to be. All that moving around makes me seasick."[5]

Viewed from the urbanized United States or Asia, such reservations seem absurd. But they're a reminder that we take for granted something extraordinary: convenient travel from one elevation to the next, with no calories expended along the way.

The convenience factor was an obvious appeal from the beginning. Within a decade of Reno getting his patent, escalators took shoppers into the highest reaches of Bon Marché in Paris, Bloomingdale's in New York, and Harrod's in London [057]. Department-store operators saw the appeal, even if early crowds were nervous about the newfangled contraption. So did subway designers. "The moving staircase is not merely an ineffable blessing to weary legs," said J.C. Martin, the engineer who installed the first elevators in the London Underground in 1911; "it is perpetual motion itself, and should be treated with reverence and gratitude" [058].[6]

Escalators were a selling point in those early years, a much-touted novelty that helped pull in shoppers [062]. But novelty goes only so far: spiral escalators were experimented with by both Reno and Charles Seeberger, who coined the word "escalator," but what caught on was Seeberger's innovation of steps as opposed to Reno's angled slats [060]. The straightforward approach is what did the trick. This was the first demonstration of one of the escalator's underlying truths: they work best when they don't require notice and they don't require thought.

Indeed, not much has changed since the early days of escalators, although there are metal steps now, instead of wooden slats or a flat rubber belt, handrails come in a variety of colors, and balustrades often boast see-through glass. Take the fifteen-second plunge into the basement level of a music or video store, and banks of televisions might broadcast images above you. Donald Trump, no shrinking violet, coated the retail escalators at his first eponymous tower in gold. And Reno and Seeberger must have raised glasses of celebration in Heaven when spiral escalators appeared at the Creo Shopping Center in Tsukuba, Japan, in 1985. A three-story spiral system debuted three years later in San Francisco. The "fantastic kinetic sculptures . . . will become a tourist attraction,"[7] predicted a bemused Allan Temko, the *San Francisco Chronicle*'s architecture critic, and he was right: "One last thing I have to mention today is the spiral escalators at the shopping center here," reports an Australian tourist in her internet diary. "Everyone has seen boring straight-line escalators, but these curve in a semi-circle as they go up or down. Impressive!"[8] [059]

Yet these "innovations" all feel like gimmicks in the end. San Francisco's spiral system, for instance, remains the only one in the United States, according to creator Mitsubishi (after all, a spokesman adds, they cost roughly ten times as much as a plain diagonal unit).[9] Other flourishes haven't even made it across the Pacific, like escalators that flatten out to create a short plateau in the middle of an ascent or descent—supposedly offering comfort to vertigo-inclined riders. Instead, functionality rules—and at a pace, truthfully, that can feel dowdy in today's ever-more-frenetic world. Consider this: the average escalator still travels at roughly 100 feet (30 meters) per minute, not so different from the pace in the 1920s. That's fine for distracted shoppers or wide-eyed tourists, but for movers-and-shakers the pace is too slow [061].

061 The first floor viewed from an escalator in Greenhut-Siegel-Cooper Company, 18-19 Streets on 6th Avenue, New York, *c.* 1912.

062 In-store advertisement for escalators at the Kaufman-Straus Department Store, Louisville, Kentucky, 1949.

Jane looks on sympathetically when George has a mishap at the factory, 1990. From *Jetsons: The Movie*, directed by Joseph Barbera and William Hanna, MCA.

Hillside people-mover at Hong Kong's Mid-levels, 1999.

A proposal by Diller + Scofidio for the Boston Institute of Contemporary Art, 2002.

So escalator etiquette evolves. Queuing didn't exist in the United States a generation ago, that practice where escalator riders content to drift stand on the right while movers-and-shakers stride by on the left. Now it's standard operating procedure in transit stations; you feel the tension when the innocent or ignorant break the rules. And if those rules are unspoken here, they're explicit elsewhere: transit systems from Tokyo to Toronto bear signs that announce "Stand Right, Walk Left" [074].

While escalators plod along, their vertical counterpart, elevators, snap in step with the times—ever more swiftly, with ever more glitz. Some models can bound upwards nearly 2500 feet (762 meters) in a minute. Glass models levitate in hotel atriums and alongside parking garages. As for the ones found in office towers, if the address is a high-rent high-rise built in the last twenty years, the cab is probably cloaked in enough marble to make a Medici swoon. Speckled handrails pale in comparison.

To see just how far Mr. Reno's endless conveyor can be stretched, look to Asia. As cities like Singapore and Tokyo develop at levels of density beyond the wildest American imagination, escalators and moving sidewalks are a key form of transit. This is particularly true in Hong Kong, where an entire hillside is conquered by the Central Mid-Levels Escalators—a 2625-foot (800-meter) collage of moving sidewalks topped by a canopy and open at the sides, lined by open-air markets and apartment towers. Since the system opened in 1993, it has become the centerpiece of the neighborhood and an alternative to automobiles [064].

Sound familiar? No wonder: this is the world imagined by nineteenth-century futurists and twentieth-century modernists [066, 067]. Nor is it far from the zippy home of the Jetsons, with sidewalks whisking George Jetson and Jane, his wife, to their destination [063]. But Americans don't want their lives shaped *that* much: people are only inclined to give up so much control of their personal movement (freeways are embraced in part because drivers can gun the engine when the coast is clear). The one secure beachhead of moving sidewalks is at airports, the larger and more horizontal the better. The rolling rubber makes vast terminals manageable but most are utilitarian to a fault, the only bit of drama the taped proclamation that "the moving sidewalk is coming to an end, please watch your step."

The great exception, of course, is the United Terminal at Chicago's O'Hare International Airport—a vivid reminder of what architects lose by ignoring the design potential of conveyance. When the terminal underwent a $500-million expansion in the mid-1980s, architect Helmut Jahn plopped a new building 870 feet (265 meters) away from its twin. How to connect them? With an underground passage tucked below the taxiing airplanes. To go from one concourse to the next is to descend the equivalent of four stories on escalators 70 feet (21 meters) long—and then be plunged into soft darkness, with ambient music hovering above two moving sidewalks in each direction. Neon sculptures by artist Michael Hayden send colors tracing back and forth [069]. "Traveling this passage is an almost surreal experience," *Chicago Tribune* architecture critic Paul Gapp wrote in 1987. "From the start, everyone knew that passing through such a long underground passage on moving sidewalks could turn out to be boring and, to some people, perhaps a bit forbidding. The solution turned out to be a piece of artistic show business."[10]

Two other architects who grasp the strange sweep of moving sidewalks and escalators are Elizabeth Diller and Ricardo Scofidio. When their New York-based firm received a public art commission for the "sterile corridor" 2200 feet (670 meters) long that takes travelers to customs at John F. Kennedy International Airport, they lined the journey with 4-foot-square video screens spaced every 22 feet (7 meters). Images of packing and unpacking quiver and

066 **Proposal for an elevated railway for New York City, by Alfred Speer, 1873.** Alfred Speer, an amateur inventor from Passaic, New Jersey, came up with an idea for an "endless travelling train" that would be driven by cables powered by steam engines.

067 OPPOSITE *King's Dream of New York*, **1895.** From Moses King, *King's New York Views*, Boston (M. King) 1895.

068 ABOVE
Travelogues at the international arrivals building,
Terminal 4, John F. Kennedy Airport, New York,
designed by Skidmore, Owings & Merrill, 2001.

069 OPPOSITE
Sky's the Limit by Michael Hayden at O'Hare
International Airport, Chicago, 1989.

070 TOP
Moving walkway at Caesar's Palace Casino, Las Vegas, designed by Wimberly Allison Tong & Goo, 1998.

071 ABOVE
A Cartveyor in the Great Indoors store, Novi, Michigan, 2001.

072 OPPOSITE
Otis escalator in a department store, first half of the twentieth century.

shift, forming a vague narrative [068]. "We pay a lot of attention to the potential of conveyances as a way of perceiving architecture and space," Diller says. "We're very interested in using escalators as a way of revealing and concealing views."

But even the cutting-edge credibility of Diller + Scofidio can do only so much in the face of tight budgets. In their original design for a waterfront home for the Institute of Contemporary Arts in Boston, the pair envisioned a single-run escalator slicing upwards through the building, popping out of the lobby into open air and then slicing across galleries [065]. The system was too expensive; they tried breaking it up, but the effect wasn't the same. "That little interruption was enough to change the feel from theatricality to feeling like a department store," sighs Diller, who opted finally for an oversized elevator with glass walls. "It could have been spectacular."

At least there's room for spectacle in Las Vegas—that strange laboratory of cultural innovation where high pedestrian counts are worshiped along with money and vicarious thrills. When the Strip became a promenade for strollers wanting to savor Venetian canals one moment and the Eiffel Tower the next, older casinos reached out to pull in as many consumers as they could. The result? At Caesar's Palace, the moving sidewalk is a theme park all by itself: there are sculpted centurions, marble arches, lush plantings, even cool misting machines as you leave the baking heat of Nevada for the sybaritic consumerism of ancient Rome. Not bad for a 275-foot (83.8-meter) journey [070].[11]

Perhaps it's no wonder that escalators are taken for granted in contemporary America: they do the same thing they did a century ago, in a world where everything else has changed. At least they've fared better than the traditional downtowns where they first filled a need—the Central Business District hasn't lived up to its name, anywhere, for a generation, and department stores are on the ropes. Even shopping malls lost their allure a decade ago: suburban consumers now spend Saturdays at power centers where big-box retailers spread out around enormous parking lots. At power centers, nobody rides an escalator through an atrium; nobody rides an escalator at all, or even does much walking. These people are in a hurry and on a mission; they drive from box to box, and grab a shopping cart at each stop.

That grinding focus on *getting things done* runs counter to one of the escalator's covert lures: a willing surrender to forces larger than yourself. The transit rider is swallowed by the commuter stream, absolutely part of the crowd. Navigating an old-fashioned department store also means giving up control, albeit in a less obvious way—maybe you're on your own, but escalators encourage you to stray from a chosen path, give in to whims, indulge yourself! It's not by accident that necessities are found on upper floors, or escalators are arranged so that shoppers must double back at each level mid-journey. "Escalators encourage *impulse buying*," explained a 1949 Otis Elevator promotional brochure, since "passengers often stray from the Escalator to look at merchandise they would otherwise never have noticed" [072].[12]

But who wants to stray in today's multi-tasking America? Who wants to give up time, stand idle on a subway escalator for forty seconds when you can hustle up or down it in twenty? From this streamlined perspective, escalators look archaic.

There are disadvantages, though. Apart from, well, pokiness, there is one big drawback: they break. As does everything else in the world, true, but it's a tribute to the importance of escalators and moving sidewalks that when you step on one and it doesn't take over from there, you feel cheated (especially if the connection from subway platform to station concourse is angled at an Alpine dimension). Worse, the flow of escalator stairs never seems conducive to walking.

There's also the possibility of bodily harm, especially in this age of long scarves and untied shoelaces. Clothing gets snagged, fingers get pinched—or worse. Thirty-one people were killed in London's King's Cross station in 1987 when a wooden-slatted escalator caught fire; as recently as 1998, a woman was strangled when her coat got caught in a moving staircase at a Washington metro station. Realistically, such occurrences are rare, but perhaps the Managua housekeeper had a point.

On the other hand, what's the alternative—slides? Climbing walls with fake rocks? So the endless conveyor waits placidly, on call wherever convenience is desired and verticality exists. Which brings us to Target, the national retailer that works overtime making thrift synonymous with hip, where you can be stylish on a shoestring budget. It's also where, as of 2002, twenty-one of the chain's 1148 stores have special escalators that pull shopping carts up or down alongside customers, from shop floor to dedicated parking [071].[13]

Nor is Target the only behemoth intrigued by this product. Ikea uses them, as do Costco and Wal-Mart. Not at every location, but even in the 'burbs there's a limit to how much land can be covered by asphalt. And whenever cars park on the roof behind a stucco cornice, or underneath the cheap luncheonette, escalators usually follow.

Besides showing yet again the escalator's genius for conforming to society's needs, these shopping-cart conveyors connect to the past in a heartening way. They show that people still have the capability to be impressed—amazed!—at what an escalator can do. Just like those first puzzled 1890s shoppers. Just like San Francisco. Just like Managua. "But enough about that. What you really want to know about is the escalators at Target, right?" columnist Jane Lotter of Seattle's *Jet City Maven* monthly asked her readers in 2000. "You've heard there are escalators for people, and you can understand that. But you've also heard there are—get this—escalators for the shopping carts. Is it true? YES! IT'S TRUE! AND IT'S HILARIOUS! . . . They'll make you laugh out loud. And if they don't then you're taking life a little too seriously, mister."[14]

Back downtown, meanwhile, old-timers sigh each time the most venerable escalators, the ones with wooden slats instead of formal stairs, are carted off to who-knows-where. They may have wobbled and creaked as they crept along, but they radiated warmth—a craftsman's pride. The last remaining wooden escalator in Boston, for instance, was a 1914 model with Vermont maple slats [073]. Alas, in 1995 it succumbed to a station renovation; the Smithsonian Institution wanted to put it on display, but logistics and reassembly costs won out over nostalgia.[15] They've nearly all gone from London's Underground, as well, and the number shrinks in North America each time a venerable department store closes or remodels.

Escalators reflect society as well as shape it, and our society strives to be more predictable and precise each year. The reaction against this seamless modernization—itself predictable, like the rise of organic food in the age of supermarkets that cover 60,000 square feet (5600 square meters)—means that for some people there's something seductive about anything attuned to the older pace. Even a rickety escalator tread, or a handrail that moves not quite in rhythm with the steps.

If Target and other big boxes are signs of the future, escalators will continue to allow for the shifting vagaries of modern life. They'll do their best to adapt. Just like the people who ride them.

073
Cleat-type double-file escalator, Park Street Subway Station, Boston, 1912.

074

Sign in Victoria Underground Station, London, 1969.

1. The Museum for the Preservation of Elevating History www.theelevatormuseum.org/e/e-4.htm, www.theelevator-museum.org.

2. Srdjan Jovanovic Weiss and Sze Tsung Leong, *"Escalator,"* *Harvard Design School Guide to Shopping*, Cologne (Taschen) 2001, p. 337.

3. "Rogers lashes out at 'tragic' £54m Pompidou Centre refit," *Architects' Journal*, January 13, 2000, p. 6.

4. Elza dos Santos, "Spring break travel to Paris: 'I could definitely live in a place like this,'" *The Flame*, vol. 1, no. 7 (April 2002). www.vic.uh.edu/flame/april2002.

5. Glenn Garvin, "Mall escalators delight, terrify Nicaraguans," *Austin American-Statesman*, February 15, 1999.

6. Ray Orton, *Moving People: From Street to Platform: 100 Years Underground*, Mobile, Alabama (Elevator World) 2001, p. 27.

7. Allan Temko, "Theatrics Packing Them In at San Francisco Center," *San Francisco Chronicle*, November 14, 1988.

8. Found in "Diary of a Witt," from the website *Fairly Tested* at www.froggy.com.au/pdavis/index.htm froggy.com.au/pdavis/diary2.htm.

9. Telephone interview with Mitsubishi official, October 2002.

10. Paul Gapp, "Oh Boy, O'Hare! At United's Terminal, Getting There is Half the Fun," *Chicago Tribune,* October 4, 1987.

11. Telephone interview with Caesar's Palace official, November 2002.

12. Brochure quoted in *Harvard Design School Guide to Shopping*, p. 354.

13. Telephone interview with Target official, October 2002.

14. Jane Lotter, "Jane Explains: Moving Target," *Jet City Maven*, vol. 4, no. 12, December 2000 (now called *The North Seattle Sun*).

15. Michael Topel, "Ancient escalator was a link to history," *The Patriot-Ledger*, April 3, 1995.

4

Hovering Vision

Phil Patton

075
Exterior of the Hyatt Regency, Atlanta, designed by
John Portman, 1967.

**"What in the world keeps this thing up in the air?" croaked Grandma
Josephine.**
"Skyhooks," said Mr. Wonka.
"You amaze me," said Grandma Josephine . . . .
Roald Dahl, *Charlie and the Great Glass Elevator*[1]

The most famous glass elevator in fiction made its appearance in 1964 when
Roald Dahl published *Charlie and the Chocolate Factory*. The most famous glass
elevator in reality took shape in blueprints at almost the same moment, as architect John Portman began planning the Hyatt Regency Hotel in Atlanta, Georgia,
which opened to the public in June 1967 [076]. Its twenty-two-story atrium and
glass elevators made the hotel an immediate and immense hit with the public.

Like Willy Wonka's elevator, held up by the mythical skyhook, John Portman's
version was suspended in the popular imagination and fantasy by a long tradition
of collective dreams of hovering, floating, and rising—and a long popular-culture
tradition in fiction, film, pulp magazines, and at world's fairs.

Visitors from the rural hinterlands around Atlanta made special trips to the city
to see the elevators. The multiple cars, some rising as others fell, were tapered
at the ends like little candies in twist wrappers and lit like miniature riverboats.

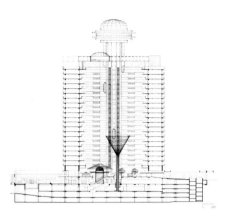

076
Plan of the Hyatt Regency, Atlanta, by John Portman, 1967.

077 TOP
View from the third-floor balcony in the Johnson Wax Building, Racine, Wisconsin, designed by Frank Lloyd Wright, 1939.

078 ABOVE
Tivoli Gardens at night, Copenhagen, Denmark.

079 OPPOSITE
Wide view of the atrium at the Hyatt Regency, Atlanta.

As a child in western North Carolina I made the trip myself, and recall enjoying the surge of imagination felt by everyone passing through the low entrance into the immense atrium. The elevator ride was worth the whole trip: a rocket launch take off, then the passage through the building's roof to the Polaris rotating restaurant, and a glimpse of the city and landscape beyond, all emerging with sudden brightness [075].

Portman's glass elevators were a sight in themselves, like vertical versions of the monorail at Disneyworld. In 1967 images of the space capsule and gantry from the space program were still fresh in people's minds, and the elevators suggested the drama of the launching pad; at the same time they provided the lobby with a focal point analogous to the wide, formal staircases found in more traditional hotels.

The elevators at the Hyatt Regency not only rose through the atrium lobby but also ascended through its ceiling, to the saucer-shaped blue-glass revolving restaurant on the top of the building. That blue disc, swelling with skylights, immediately reminded visitors of the saucer-like structure atop Seattle's 1962 Space Needle, and became a signature of the Atlanta skyline. It was called Polaris—the name not only of the North Star but also of the nation's first sea-launched intercontinental ballistic missile. The menus of the rotating restaurant were shaped like the elevators, and local businesses used the shape in advertising as a signature image for the city.

Riders on the elevators passed exotic plants hung from the balconies and looked down on several restaurants [079]. An abstract metal sculpture roofed the Parasol lounge and—most famous of the tales visitors carried home to the small towns of the South—there were huge cages of exotic birds, whose calls filled the air.

"The last time we saw Charlie, he was riding high above his hometown in the Great Glass Elevator . . . ."

John Portman was born in Atlanta in 1924 and studied architecture at the Georgia Institute of Technology. As a student, like many of his generation, he was inspired by Frank Lloyd Wright, whose interior spaces—the Larkin Building, Johnson Wax, and the Guggenheim—are clear ancestors of Portman's lobby [077, 080]. During travels in Europe, Portman was impressed with Le Corbusier, especially the church at Ronchamp, but came back with a deep impression of another sort: Tivoli Gardens in Copenhagen. "It is a very happy place," he recalled. "Everyone was smiling. Disney got a lot of ideas from Tivoli" [078]. After graduation in 1950, he apprenticed for three years with the Atlanta firm of Stevens and Wilkinson before striking out on his own. His first projects were schools and small business buildings. He shrewdly perceived that in go-go Atlanta an architect's best client was himself. He became a developer, converting a parking garage into a furniture display space.

Beginning in 1963, he conceived plans for what became the Hyatt, a rethinking of the urban hotel. Ground was broken in mid-1964, a neat century after Sherman's burning of the city; but it was not until 1966 that the Pritzker family and the Hyatt Hotels Corporation bought into the project, which had initially been developed in cooperation with Trammel Crow, the powerful Texas corporation.

In an interview in 2002, Portman was at pains to emphasize that the glass elevator idea grew from the wider project of "taking apart and reassembling" the basic hotel of the time—in order to create a larger, internal space. "Because space is at a premium in the city, the atrium would offer refreshment to those who came from the street."

"We were using the elevators as a key element; the elevator really established the dynamics of the whole space." Making circulation the dramatic key to a

080 **Looking skyward in the atrium of the Solomon R. Guggenheim Museum, New York, designed by Frank Lloyd Wright, 1959.**

081
Elevator cab at 49 Wall Street, New York, 1932.

082 ABOVE
Elevators in the atrium of the Hyatt Regency, Atlanta, designed by John Portman, 1967.

083 OPPOSITE
Elevator at the Embarcadero Center, San Francisco, designed by John Portman, 1987.

space is a tried-and-true architectural strategy—think of buildings as disparate as the Laurentian Library in Florence, with Michelangelo's dramatic, virtuoso composition of cascading stairs, or Morris Lapidus's melodramatic curving lobby stairs at the Fontainebleau Hilton in Miami. The Guggenheim Museum's spiraling ramps, more circulation than galleries, are the heart of its design. Only the substitution of elevator and escalator, of mechanical means of circulation for the traditional variety—the staircase—is relatively new. In true modernist style, Portman sought motion. "To pull the elevators out of the wall made them like moving seats in a theater," he said. "It was like a ride for people in the elevator; it was like a kinetic sculpture for those sitting and watching."

There was naturally concern that some visitors would become fearful inside the elevators, so Portman and his colleagues arranged the cars so there was space for fearful riders to stand against the back wall. They also provided two closed elevators in addition to the five glass capsules. Portman argues, however, that the psychological experience offered by the glass elevator was preferable to that of the traditional one. "Prior to this, the elevator was really a closed telephone booth [081]. We noticed how people respond to the closed elevator. They don't talk to each other, they just look at the floor. On the glass elevator there is continuous conversation."

Otis Elevator Company was approached about building the special cars. "Otis was really excited about it," Portman recalled. "We visited the Otis factory in New Jersey to view a mock-up of one of the cars. They had done everything we expected." The cars had neither front nor back, so the "shape had to be a capsule . . . . It had to be consistent in either direction with no differentiated top or bottom. We used the lighting to help get the proportions right [083]. That was very important; the elevators set the scale and we had to be sure that the scale inside the atrium was correct." "It's all about lights," he added. "The Tivoli lights [the small lights accenting the shape of the cars] were important."

Of the atrium, Portman said, "We wanted to awaken all the senses so there was music, fountains, and birds. We wanted to integrate nature into the city; we wanted to become the living room of the city. It was a very special experience." There were also several restaurants in the space, including Kafe København, an homage to Tivoli and the Danish city Portman so enjoyed.

Portman's vision was rewarded with the hotel's tremendous popularity. On one Sunday shortly after it opened, 15,000 people filed through for a look. Emerging into the central space elicited such expressions of amazement, even from Atlanta church ladies, that the area was soon nicknamed "profanity corner." The metal ribs and lights of the elevators evoked the riverboats with fluted smokestacks from Currier & Ives and Southern mythology [082]. Diane Thomas of the *Atlanta Constitution* wrote that the elevators looked "like enormous diving bells full of people" and quoted one guest who declared them better than any ride at Coney Island.[2]

Life and *Time* magazines ran celebratory articles with photographs. The architect Edward Durrell Stone flew into Atlanta, took a taxi from the airport to the new hotel, marched into the lobby to view the atrium, then promptly returned to the waiting taxi and reversed his journey.

"My Elevator is air-conditioned, ventilated, aerated and automated in every possible way."

The hotel turned into a symbol of Atlanta and the Sunbelt cities that had risen up as quickly as it had.[3] "As a symbol it was an enormous boost to the city at the time," Portman said later.

Atlanta has always been the capital of the New South—of many new Souths, actually. Serving a vast hinterland that was desperate for a focal point, Atlanta

084 TOP
Decorative metalwork for passenger lift in a stairwell, Berlin, 1910. From Kerstin and Alfred Englert, *Lifts in Berlin*, Berlin (Jovis) 1998.

085 CENTER
Ferris wheel at the World's Columbian Exposition, Chicago, 1893. From James W. Shepp and Daniel B. Shepp, *Shepp's World's Fair Photographed*, Chicago (Globe Bible Publishing Co.) 1893.

086 ABOVE
"Trade Your Trouble for a Bubble," the back cover of an issue of *Amazing Stories,* **1946.** From Joseph J. Corn and Brian Horrigan, *Yesterday's Tomorrows: Past Visions of the American Future*, Baltimore (Johns Hopkins University Press) 1996.

087 OPPOSITE
The Bradbury Building, Los Angeles, designed by George H. Wyman, 1893.

has torn itself down to rebuild itself many times. It has a history if reinventing itself: the phoenix is its emblem, evoking the city arising from the ashes left by Sherman's march. But this in itself is a myth: there wasn't much to Atlanta before Sherman. Before the Civil War, the city was not known as Atlanta, but as "Terminus," an apt name for a municipality made important by the coincidence of railroad crossings. The site of a world exposition in the late nineteenth century, it was already billing itself as a symbol of the New South. Its later prosperity was built on its airport, on interstate crossings, and its role as trade and convention center for much of the South.

By the 1960s, billing itself as "the city too busy to hate," and as the home of Dr. Martin Luther King, Jr., Atlanta strove to rise above the image of the racially divided South that was beamed into American homes on television news. Portman was one of those who helped found Forward Atlanta, a planning and promotional organization, in 1960. The usual round of urban redevelopment was followed by the construction of new stadiums and convention centers. By 1970, Atlanta was the center of the New South; in the eyes of the media, it was "Hotlanta," a modern and innovative city that in 1976 gave the country a president. Jimmy Carter's election was seen as marking the long-delayed end of reconstruction and a symbolic restoration of the South to the rest of the country. Atlanta's own reconstruction was the visible analogue of this political process.

"The elevator shuddered and then with a fearful whooshing noise it shot vertically upward like a rocket."

In 1972 Roald Dahl brought the glass elevator at Mr. Wonka's chocolate factory to the fore in *Charlie and the Great Glass Elevator*, the sequel to *Charlie and the Chocolate Factory*. Flying off into orbit, Mr. Wonka's elevator docks with a space hotel. It becomes, in effect, a spaceship itself.

Portman's elevators were also Space Age, mixed with Old South. The Hyatt Regency elevators would not have been so well received without the existence of a long fascination in popular culture with the idea of the glass elevator. In speculative magazines and science-fiction films, the idea of the glass elevator was not unlike that of the monorail, a clichéd feature of visions of the city of the future, their bullet-like cars suspended from overhead rails.

Before the glass elevator, the open-cage elevator offered a similar sensation of being suspended in air [084]. Whether on the Eiffel Tower or fitted into the stairwells of apartment houses, the open-cage elevator for many Americans was exotic and European; but Portman's elevators also had precedent in the Ferris wheel car. The first Ferris Wheel was erected at the 1893 World's Columbian Exposition in Chicago [085]. The mobility of the Ferris wheel, employing engineering in the service of spectacle, is often contrasted with the static papier-mâché neoclassical buildings of the fair's "White City."

Another precedent that Portman himself points out is the Bradbury Building in Los Angeles. This astonishing structure, designed by George Wyman, was built around a five-story atrium where stairs are supplemented by elevators with open cages, their mechanisms proudly displayed like a kinetic sculpture. The interior space is lined with balconies and doors of frosted glass, in whose offices one imagines private investigators at work [087].[4]

Science-fiction visions from the 1930s onwards are full of exotic transportation schemes and future technologies in which transparency played a large role. *Things to Come*, the 1936 film by William Menzies based on the novel by H.G. Wells, with sets partly designed by Bauhaus veteran László Moholy-Nagy, is famed for its glass elevators: passenger cars with clear walls shoot across the scenery like messages through a Paris pneumatique.[5] The underground city of

113

088 **The "Travolator" connecting the El Cortez Hotel to the Travolator Motor Hotel, San Diego, 1959.**

089 OPPOSITE **Vision of a futuristic city from the 1936 film** *Things to Come*, **directed by William Cameron Menzies.**

the film's utopian future is as windowless as a Portman atrium space, has similar balconies, and features escalators and monorails as well as the elevators [089].

In 1946, the pulp magazine *Amazing Stories* depicted a miniature city constructed inside a giant transparent sphere that rolled across the landscape on a sort of elevated highway. "Trade your trouble for a bubble" intoned the head-line [086].[6] In 1979 Arthur C. Clarke, father of the communications satellite and author of *2001: A Space Odyssey* (1968), expanded on the space-elevator idea as a serious proposal for getting men and material from Earth into space.[7] In the 1960s "Space Age," rethinking the elevator as a capsule was an appropriate response to a time when the first astronauts were being carried to their own capsules on top of rockets by openwork elevators in the gantries at Cape Canaveral [090].

A clear precedent for the Hyatt was the Space Needle, the signature building of the Century 21 World's Fair in Seattle in 1962, 600 feet (180 meters) high and topped with an observation floor and revolving restaurant [093]. Less well known, but also at the fair, was a clear plastic spherical elevator called the Bubbleator, in which guides dressed in silver space suits led visitors on "tours of the future." Inside, guests saw visions of the atomic and space future in the "World of Tomorrow" exhibit. In all, 2.5 million people rode the Bubbleator [091].[8]

In 1956, another glass hotel elevator was built, the Starlight Express in San Diego. It was an exterior elevator, added to the 1927 El Cortez Hotel by owner Harry Handley. It is discussed in Kyle E. Ciani and Cynthia Malinick's article "From Spanish Romance to Neon Confidence and Demolition Fear: The Twentieth-Century Life of the El Cortez Hotel."[9] To attract resort visitors back to San Diego's downtown, Ciani and Malinick report, Handlery had built a swimming pool in the hotel in 1952; in 1956 he added a ballroom, the Starlight Room, on the twelfth floor. As with the Hyatt Regency, these catered to "a new kind of client, the business traveler in for a convention or sales meeting."

The Starlight Express carried visitors from the hotel's lobby to the Starlight Room and on up to the Sky Room on the fifteenth floor [092]. "Designed by C.J. 'Pat' Paderewski, the elevator was only the second operational glass exterior elevator in the world," Ciani and Malinick declared. The Starlight Express emulated the design of early elevators and used a hydraulic rather than a cable system. A hydraulic ram one foot (30 centimeters) in diameter, driven by electrically powered pumps, pushed the elevator car up the side of the hotel. The ram retracted into a cylinder 175 feet (53 meters) deep as the car descended to the lobby. Neither of the major elevator manufacturers, Otis or Westinghouse, would build the system, so Paderewski found a local firm, Elevator Electric Inc., to construct and install it. "Two rails held the cab in place," they report, "and neon stars decorated the enameled metal in between the elevator rails." Three years later, the article says, Paderewski went on to design an escalator billed as the "Travolator" that presented a view of the city while carrying pedestrians from the El Cortez to the Travolator Motor Hotel, a motel and parking garage across the street [088]. (The TRAV-O-LATOR had been invented by Otis Elevator Company in 1955 and is featured in their bulletin of the same year.)

The Starlight Express became a local landmark, serving as a site for promotional stunts and social events. "Absolutely exciting," one San Diegan remembered. "One enjoyed the most spectacular view of the city from the elevator, especially at night." Ciani and Malinick quote a local student, Daisy Burns Munchtando, whose description of her experience riding the elevator (written at the time it was opened) won her first place in a writing contest:

"Sixteen of us stepped into sheer outer space. This was the maximum load and we were counted. We hung suspended in mid-air in a clear glass cage as we slowly climbed up the front of the building. Subdued lighting and

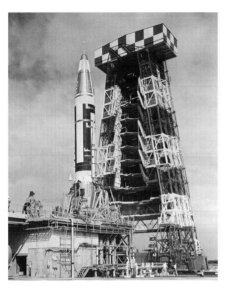

090 TOP
Missile and gantry tower at Cape Canaveral, Florida, 1958.

091 OPPOSITE
The Bubbleator inside the Washington State Coliseum during the World's Fair, Seattle, 1964.

092
The El Cortez Hotel, San Diego, designed by Albert R. Walker and Percy Eisen, 1927, showing C.J. Paderewski's Starlight Express elevator, added in 1956.

093 Edward E. Carlson's Space Needle and the Monorail engineered by the Alweg Company, both designed for the World's Fair, Seattle, 1962.

soft 'piped-in' music produced a feeling of luxurious unreality. There was complete silence lest someone break the spell. The verbose had lost voice, overwhelmed by the magic fairyland of the soundless city far below."

Inspiring such emotions was also Portman's goal and the appeal extended far beyond Atlanta or San Diego (whose elevator he doesn't recall ever seeing). He found himself in demand, and the elevators in the Hyatt Regency were followed by those in other hotels designed on a similar model. It was a popular formula in what was coming to be known as the Sunbelt. Portman was called to cities that wanted to re-create downtowns. The Bonaventure Hotel in Los Angeles, the Embarcadero Center in San Francisco, and the Renaissance Center in Detroit are huge developments that combine hotels with offices and retail space [096]. By the 1970s, Paul Gapp, architecture critic of the *Chicago Tribune*, called Portman "the most influential architect in America."

While appearing modern, even futuristic, Portman's style also shared the theatrical qualities of earlier hotels, with their people-watching opportunities, from the Peabody in Memphis to the Plaza in New York. Robert A.M. Stern has linked the Portman hotels to an American tradition of hotel lobbies as huge interior public spaces. In *Pride of Place* (1986) he describes what is possibly the ultimate Portman space, Detroit's Renaissance Center, where

"the public spaces . . . consist of a kinetic maze of ramps, escalators, and 'pods' accessible by spiral staircases and exposed elevators. To wander from the neutral 'people scoops' of corridors to the multilevel histrionics of the eight-story atrium is to stumble forward into the future of Buck Rogers's twenty-fifth century and the fantastic past of Tarzan's jungle, while to ride on its elevators is to travel from backward into degree zero to Alphaville."[10]

But observers soon noted that the later buildings lacked the detail of the Hyatt Regency, and their elevators did not have the show-biz "Southern" style of the original. The trade-off Portman boasted of as the key to his formula—sacrificing fine finish and materials for expansive space—made the Renaissance Center, the Bonaventure, and the Hyatt Regency O'Hare look like cavernous, crude, concrete, steel, and glass silos [094, 095].

By the 1980s, Atlanta's New South image—and the public perception of Portman's own vision—had frozen into caricature. Critics of Sunbelt sprawl and the lack of downtowns criticized Portman's developments, saying they were "turning away" from the city and the life of the street and finding them instead to be deadly spaces. Portman's designs were widely criticized by commentators such as James Howard Kunstler, author of *The Geography of Nowhere* (1993) and other attacks on American cityscapes and sprawl.[11] Kunstler called the Hyatt Regency "an inside-out building that rejects the surrounding street and attempts to compensate with a seven-hundred-foot-high [*sic*] indoor atrium, along which elevators climb like the projectiles in a theme park thrill ride. But rather than make people feel grand, the outlandish atrium only made them feel small." Kunstler grows a bit hysterical in adding, "it was so overwhelming that it induced vertigo, agoraphobia, and panic attacks."[12]

This darker side to the experience of the interior spaces and elevators of the Sunbelt, as well as to the political and economic systems that built them, was sharply caricatured in William Diehl's *Sharky's Machine* (1978), the bestselling novel made into a film with Burt Reynolds. The novel's villain builds a hotel that sounds like an exaggerated version of the Hyatt Regency. Its atrium is filled with a jungle of plants and buildings and a mad theme park with an Asian focus. There is a thrill ride like a giant pachinko machine. Guests climb into balls—downsized versions of the giant *Amazing Stories* bubble towns—and bounce along ramps.

094 TOP
The Bonaventure Hotel, Los Angeles, designed by John Portman, 1977.

095 ABOVE
The Renaissance Center, Detroit, designed by John Portman, 1976.

096 OPPOSITE
The atrium of the Embarcadero Center, San Francisco, designed by John Portman, 1974.

097 TOP
View of Peachtree Center, Atlanta, in 1986, showing the Polaris restaurant designed by John Portman, 1967.

Over the last thirty years, the Atlanta skyline has grown considerably taller. The original Hyatt and the Polaris restaurant are now dwarfed in comparison to the rest of Peachtree Center.

098 ABOVE
Elevator at The Mall, Short Hills, New Jersey.

099 OPPOSITE
Elevator in the Prada Store, SoHo, New York, designed by Rem Koolhaas, 2001.

In the lobby, the elevators are "glass and copper bullets attached to the side of the lobby."[13]

Tom Wolfe, in *A Man in Full*, his 1998 novel about an Atlanta real-estate developer, caricatures the zealous world of downtown Atlanta. In a mock epic catalog of the buildings of the Atlanta skyline, contemplated from his private airplane by Charlie Croker, the hero, Portman is even mentioned by name:

"In the distance the sun was exploding off the towers of Downtown and Midtown Atlanta and the commercial swath on the eastern side of Buckhead. Charlie knew them all by sight. He knew them not by the names of their architects—what were architects but neurotic and 'artistic' hired help?—but by the names of their developers. There was John Portman's seventy-story glass cylinder, the Westin Peachtree Plaza, flashing in the sun. (Portman was smart; he was his own architect.)"[14]

By the time Wolfe was writing, the original Hyatt had long since been dwarfed by the addition of two towers of rooms and by other buildings in Peachtree Center. The lobby sculpture had been removed and the blue saucer on the roof almost lost among the taller towers of downtown Atlanta [097].

But by the turn of the millennium, perhaps as part of the renewed appreciation for the 1960s and 1970s, and out of growing impatience with overly abstract and theoretical architecture, things were changing. Portman's hotels seemed about to enjoy that sort of reappraisal that Morris Lapidus's over-the-top, festive Miami Beach hotels have recently undergone.

While smaller versions of Portman's glass elevator have become a cliché of hotel and shopping-mall design—a typical effort in the Short Hills Mall, New Jersey, serves as a "focus feature"—the magic of the glass elevator remains vital [098]. Today when retailing and entertainment are joined, escalators and elevators are part of the sales show. The same elevator-and-transparent-tube scheme of *Things to Come* was realized in a strange place: Niketown stores, where it moves shoeboxes around. The effect is part Pompidou Center, part Jetsons. In Manhattan, Prada's SoHo store, designed by Rem Koolhaas and opened in 2001, features a massive, room-sized, cylindrical glass elevator lined with metal benches for riders. Placed at its center is a display for products on sale in the store. Even though it only moves between two floors, the Prada elevator has become as much a tourist sight as Portman's original glass elevators in Atlanta [099].

Despite the abundance of mundane glass elevators in shopping malls and suburban hotels, the magical vision of a floating glass bubble continues to fascinate. Like the skyhook, like the future, like the sky itself, the *dream* of the glass elevator remains ever elusive.

123

1. All quoted material in the subtitles is taken from Roald Dahl, *Charlie and the Great Glass Elevator*, New York (Knopf) 1972; reissued New York (Puffin) 1998, pp. 1, 2, 4, 83.

2. Diane Thomas, "Walk Into the Lobby, Look Up ... Bet You'll Say Something," *Atlanta Constitution*, June 25, 1967, p. 22, column 1.

3. The Sunbelt refers to the band of southern and western American states that prospered in the 1970s.

4. The Bradbury Building can also be seen in *Blade Runner* (1982), Ridley Scott's "grunge sci-fi" film with sets by Syd Mead.

5. *Things to Come*, director William Cameron Menzies, 1936, London Film Productions.

6. Joseph J. Corn and Brian Horrigan, *Yesterday's Tomorrows: Past Visions Of The American Future,* Baltimore (The Johns Hopkins University Press), 1984.

7. Arthur C. Clarke, *2001: A Space Odyssey*, New York (New American Library) c. 1968.

8. The Bubbleator was eventually sold to private citizens who turned it into a huge terrarium.

9. Kyle E. Ciani and Cynthia Malinick, "From Spanish Romance to Neon Confidence and Demolition Fear: The Twentieth-Century Life of the El Cortez Hotel" in *The Journal of San Diego History*, Winter 2000, vol. 46, no. 1.

10. Robert A.M. Stern, *Pride of Place*, Boston (Houghton Mifflin) and New York (American Heritage) 1986.

11. James Howard Kunstler, *The Geography of Nowhere*, New York (Simon & Schuster) c. 1993.

12. James Howard Kunstler, *The City in Mind*, New York (Free Press) c. 2001, pp. 63–64.

13. William Diehl, *Sharky's Machine*, New York (Delacorte Press) c. 1978, p. 92.

14. Tom Wolfe, *A Man in Full*, Rockland, Massachusetts (Wheeler Publishing) 1998, p. 63.

5

Conveyance "Germs": Elevators, Automated Vehicles, and the Shape of Global Cities

Keller Easterling

Spectators viewing a model city from a conveyor at the Futurama Exhibit, World's Fair, New York, 1939.

The elevator is a special prop for the imagination. It is the box from which one "enters a room briskly" in science fiction. In the classic science-class exposition, it is used to illustrate the general theory of relativity. As the *axis mundi* that moves between concentric rings of gravitational pull, or between orders of organization or power, the elevator has a role in the scenarios of philosophy and futurology. Futuristic projections feature nanotechnological structures that reach from Earth to satellites, and which are even called "elevators." In fiction and cinema, the elevator is the site of wordless embarrassment or cool and final goodbyes, not prolonged hanky-waving farewells. It is a black box that erases notions of scale, external points of reference, and sometimes, in our imagination, memory, time, or distance.

Of all the imaginings associated with the elevator, one extreme vision has already become reality. Elevators, as the "germs" or technological imperatives that can determine a skyscraper's height and footprint, have travelled through urban fields with the speed of an epidemic, making, in less than a half century, cities grow in block after block of towers.[1] It is not adherence to a single visionary design, but the incremental adoption of a germ (*i.e.* the genetics of an invention) that has shaped a species of global city.

Futurama Exhibit at the World's Fair, New York, 1939.

Yet perhaps the most persistent—and as-yet-unfulfilled—ambition linked to this vision of the "conveyance germ" is one that is shared by vehicles of all types and that has the potential to generate further new types of urban development. It is the dream of movement not only up and down but omnidirectional—automated movement that is instantly responsive to need, like a biological circulatory system or an electronic network [102]. Historically, vehicles ranging from elevators to conveyor belts to cars have aspired to these models, which include the concept not only of movement but also of navigation. Cars have sometimes been conceived on the model of the elevator, as a type of vehicle that moves intelligently through buildings and infrastructures; elevators have occasionally been designed to replicate cars' ability to move horizontally, independent of a single shaft. Automated guided vehicles (AGVs) of all sorts combine the functions and characteristics of elevators, cars, cranes, lifts, and other lateral moving vehicles. Any of these vehicles, aspiring to ever-greater navigational intelligence, has the potential to reshape expectations about what constitutes navigable surface in architecture and urban planning.

Significant inventions that do not receive mainstream government or institutional research support are often developed at the eccentric edges of private sponsorship, or in another experimental testing ground, moving several times between edge and center before becoming part of mainstream manufacturing and design. Such inventions can be found in many fields, from warfare to amusement parks, from the noses of airplanes to girdles to golf clubs to automobiles.[2] Today the testing grounds of new automated conveyance devices for freight and passenger transport are the gigantic conurbations of warehouses and logistics installations—spaces for processing people and objects in transit— clustering around ports and airports.

Moreover, these new devices act as the germs from which develop the "software" and "hardware" of a new species of global urbanism: the logistics city. If the global city as financial center is organized vertically by the elevator, the global city as logistics center is organized horizontally by automated devices that handle material from container transshipment. From New York to São Paulo to Tokyo, the elevator generated the skyscraper urbanism of the financial city. From Singapore to Rotterdam to Alliance, Texas, automated devices generate the horizontal conurbations of the logistics city, the free economic zones handling complex movements of people, vehicles, goods, and information [121].

The Futurama exhibition at the 1939 World's Fair in New York City staged the first dramatizations of the dream of omnidirectional automated conveyance. A circular ring of seating slowly rotated around the central model, gradually revealing the projected rural and urban landscape of 1960 [101]. In this air-conditioned, slowly moving, darkened room, the illusion was of smooth continuous movement, an auto-ballet on a web of roadways, spreading horizontally everywhere:

"This superb one-directional highway with its seven lanes . . . at designated speeds of 50, 75 and 100 miles per hour is engineered for easy grades and for speed with safety. . . . Traffic moves at unreduced rates of speed. Safe distance between cars is maintained by automatic radar control. Curb sides assist the driver in keeping his car in the proper lane under all circumstances."[3] [100]

In the film that accompanied the show, *To New Horizons,* organ music appropriate for a soap opera was matched by the equally lugubrious voice-over, in which the narrator held, almost sang, the deep tones, briefly hitting selected phrases with a note of breathless enthusiasm. He described Corbusian cities with rooftop landing pads for helicopters and autogyros set amidst spectacular

The S B Curve Conveyor System, 2001.

103 OPPOSITE
Volkswagen Car Tower, Wolfsburg, Germany, 2000.
From *Elevator World*, November 2001.

Another intersection between cars and elevators is the automatic garage. Here a fully automated elevator system lifts, lowers, and parks cars for storage.

104
The ULTra Vehicle, 2000, near Bristol, England.

scenic landscapes of greenhouse agriculture, all connected by a spreading web of open roads.[4]

While Futurama was supposedly the visionary model for America's mid-century Interstate Highway system, it was different in at least one important respect: its cars were automated, radio-controlled vehicles that, like elevators, were dispatched from place to place. Futurama inspired subsequent, heavily funded research in the automobile and aerospace industries into automated transport systems. In the ultimate dream, cars would become dual transport vehicles, joining or separating according to the whims of the passengers, getting through the congestion of the city as mass transit and then morphing into individual, personal vehicles that delivered passengers to their front door [104]. Bruno Latour's "scientifiction" *Aramis or the Love of Technology* recounts the irrational romance of the most rational scientists with these dual transport or personal transport systems, which continued to run up against impossible complexities, yet continued to receive optimistic funding.[5]

Both the elevator and the car aspired to the condition of automation. Yet, while the elevator eventually shed its operator, experiments to create a system of driverless vehicles did not succeed so quickly.[6] Elevators and cars were considered to be entirely separate means of conveyance, in uncompetitive fields. No one longed to own their own elevator cabs, and, more importantly, the engineering of elevators differed significantly from the engineering of traffic.

Elevators were treated as a category of vehicle that operated both independently and in concert. They were timed, synchronized, and logistically arranged as a theater of access and ascent. While it is extremely complicated to devise a single algorithm for distributing hundreds of people through a skyscraper for ten hours each day, a fleet of elevators can, as in robotics, handle a large number of simple activities with slight variations [103]. Highway traffic, on the other hand, was treated as a single river, a single flow of statistics on a single network attempting to maintain a nearly constant speed and experience. Even though its millions of individual trips and destinations made it extremely complex, highway design was based on a mistaken principle that the network could be managed by enlarging the system in relation to statistical volumes of traffic. As it was established by legislation in 1956, the Interstate Highway system was not only unresponsive to its own organizational complexity, but it also failed to incorporate either the means to automation or the ability to interface with rail, ocean-going vessels, and aircraft.[7]

Ironically, concurrent with the legislation of the Interstate Highway System, two eccentric experiments in New Jersey and South Carolina introduced conveyance prototypes that would eventually contribute to the revival of the very transport ambitions that the highway system had deferred. In 1956 Malcolm McLean of Sealand, a cargo shipping company, introduced the idea of a transferable container that could be moved from a rail car to the back of a truck, and on to an ocean-going vessel [105, 106]. Even though obstructed by the railroads and the Interstate Commerce Commission, McLean pursued the project as a private venture and launched the first transatlantic container vessel in 1967, the USS *Fairland*. Containerization is a form of automation, in that it eliminates a good deal of the manual labor associated with unloading individual boxes and crates from ships and railroad cars. In 1954, two years before the advent of the container, the Cravens Company at Mercury Motor Express of South Carolina installed the first automated guided vehicle (AGV) in its factory. A guide wire installed in the factory ceiling directed a tractor that delivered to different positions on the production line.[8] These two inventions, the container and the AGV, would inform new concepts of urban logistics that may yet lead to parallel developments in passenger transportation.

105 ABOVE
**Moving a container aboard the *Ideal-X*, Port Newark,
New Jersey, 1957.**

In 1956, *Ideal-X* was the first vessel to provide scheduled
containership service in the world.

106 OPPOSITE
**On board the Maersk-Sealand container vessel *Sealand
Virginia*, Bremerhaven, Germany, 2001.**

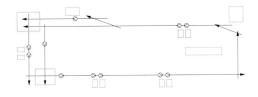

107 TOP
Moving containers at Rotterdam Port, The Netherlands, 2002.

108 CENTER
The Vertical Reciprocating Conveyor.

109 ABOVE
Map of a vehicle route, 1995.

Each vehicle has an electronic map of the environment through which it must pass. With this map the vehicle can plan the quickest route from A to B.

110 OPPOSITE
Container ship off the coast of Southern California, 2001.

While difficult to inaugurate as a mode of highway transit, automated conveyance was much easier to deploy in the world of "materials handling." Since the 1970s, the explosive growth of global trade and the intermodality between ocean, rail, and road freight containers and their vehicles have resulted in their own kinds of traffic jams. Now over 95% of the world's freight is carried on the sea, and volume is growing exponentially [110].[9] The stacking and sorting needed to move containers from ships, and pallets from warehouses are performed with increasingly high expectations of efficiency. Unlike the single flow of highway traffic, the points of transfer at terminals are differentials, or spatial gears, that must translate between one mode of transit and another. These transport chains, with their repetitive, modular problems, match the algorithmic capacities of automated control vehicles much more easily. In a bid to replace or enhance labor, automation devices become more than labor or cogs in the machinery, and resemble chips or bits in an information landscape.

Rotterdam was the first port to receive Sealand cargo ships, and it is also among those that are pursuing the next stages of port automation and sophisticated materials handling. Rotterdam's Delta-Sealand terminal now has more than fifty cranes and one hundred automated vehicles.[10] In order to compete with the relatively cheap labor of the stevedores, the system must operate twenty-four hours a day. Automated cranes remove containers from the ship and place them on waiting vehicles that, after receiving cargo, continue gliding along at 6.8 miles (11 kilometers) per hour to another stacking crane, ship, truck, or railway [107]. Transponders in the pavement and a remote monitoring system provide control facilities, but otherwise the vehicles and their cargo are the only citizens of this 0.62-mile (1-kilometer) long terminal.[11] In the late 1980s, under the theme of "Plant with a Future," "Caterpillar Inc. . . . embarked upon a massive modernization program. . . . From this engineering effort emerged a concept for automatically handling large subassembles and containers corresponding to intermodal container specification."[12] The movement of containers is just the first stage in an extended and carefully choreographed dance of storage and retrieval that descends in scale to the pallet and the individual unit for sale. The supply chain generates series of specialized warehouses that act as intermediaries between the port and further distribution, not only organizing a field of containers but sorting the contents of the containers.

The warehouse has long been a test ground for almost every sort of conveyance device. Just as large areas of outdoor space can be transformed into a machine, the warehouse is becoming not merely a building to house automatic devices but an automatic building. Storage and retrieval devices ride along the floor and transfer materials to and from pallet racks extending several stories in height [108]. Pallet forklifts, intricate networks of belt and skate-wheel conveyors, horizontal and vertical carousels of stacked racks and drawers, tractor trains, hoists, robotic gantries, and AGVs of all kinds constantly redistribute the contents of the box.

Just as an elevator shaft is a navigable infrastructural element in the skyscraper, the floor is a navigable infrastructural surface for the warehouse. More than merely part of the physical structure, it is the map that stores one half of an intelligent navigation system [117]. Whereas guide wires in the floor or ceiling used to be the chief navigational guides for automated warehouse vehicles, some companies now locate the computational intelligence in a vehicle that is able to "read" the floor [109]. FROG (Free Ranging on Grid) is one such company designing automated vehicles for industry, transport, and entertainment. The internal mapping system uses steering angle and wheel rotation odometry to measure distance traveled, occasionally double-checking the course against detectors in the floor or changes in the floor pattern.[13]

Logisticians are interested in the relationships between groups of activities in a supply chain. Such logistics, like a more complex form of horizontal elevatoring, involve designing not only the physical mechanisms of conveyance but also the intelligence that controls them. The system software is treated as a property, and the time spent in contact with the system is sold as a commodity. Transport brokers sell to potential customers the equivalent of transport timeshares or "capacity slots."[14] Both physically and functionally, an automatic warehouse resembles a computing unit or motherboard with its own area of retrievable storage, a set of communication pathways, and an area of central intelligence [111].

The development of the logistics city draws together fields of container-handling, warehouses, and international ports and airports into a legal space that usually offers twenty-four-hour customs clearance and status as a free economic zone or an export-processing zone [114]. Much more than being merely part of the infrastructure at the perimeter of familiar global cities, these large conurbations are themselves global cities. One proposal for Hong Kong, for instance, characterizes it as a logistics city, rather than a "Silicon Valley" style global city or a financial capital such as New York City, London, Tokyo, or São Paulo.[15]

"We have now moved beyond the simplistic arguments between, on the one hand, a 'Silicon Valley' replica and on the other, a financial centre. Instead there has now emerged, we believe, a consensus that Hong Kong should position itself as the world-class city of Asia by, inter alia, making better and more sophisticated use of technology. The latter should not be developed for its own sake but as an important ingredient in the integral development of Hong Kong as a world city. If all the above developments are put together, we believe a strong case can be made of developing Hong Kong into the world's leading logistic hub of a global scale."[16] [112]

Like other types of global city, the logistics city may be more firmly connected to other global cities in its network than to local conditions. Most such cities usually identify their location not in terms of place names but rather in terms of a global infrastructure that may even secede from local conditions.

In logistics patois, "park" is an enclave formation. One such enclave formation is the logistics park, or "distripark," which may range in size from a few acres to many square miles and may include office space, call centers, information technology functions, or export processing that takes advantage of cheap labor to perform a deadening task or translate a product from one organizational regime to another. Logistics parks, with their varied programs, often introduce the human element back into the interior of the automated field. Singapore's Keppel Distripark, for instance, is one of these new warm pools of logistics urbanism, reintroducing human civilization in the form of office space and a cafeteria serving Muslim, Chinese, and Indian cuisine.[17] Special automated guide vehicles also carry passenger managers and overseeing businessmen. These vehicles resemble clear plastic cylinders on wheels with an interior handrail. Standing in this safety bubble, visitors to the installation may progress through the same slow choreography as the freight vehicles, enabling them to make tours and inspections of even hazardous manufacturing or materials-handling installations.

In other park conurbations, too, freight transport technologies are returning to passenger applications and recombining with existing transport experiments [113]. For instance, in addition to automated factories, warehouses, and container terminals, FROG proposes that its logistics vehicles could be used as personal rapid transport prototypes. Experiments in this field are being undertaken in enclave formations between Schiphol and the port of Rotterdam. FROG's AGVs have been used to transport passengers from Schiphol airport to a long-stay parking lot, from a public transport hub to a business park, and to a special

111 TOP
Overhead bridges linking up the container storage system with the main terminal building, Hong Kong Air Cargo Terminal, c. 2001.

112 CENTER
Hong Kong Air Cargo Terminal, c. 2001.

113 ABOVE
Automated guided vehicles, c. 2002.

114 OPPOSITE
Container stacking area at the Port of Long Beach, California, 2001.

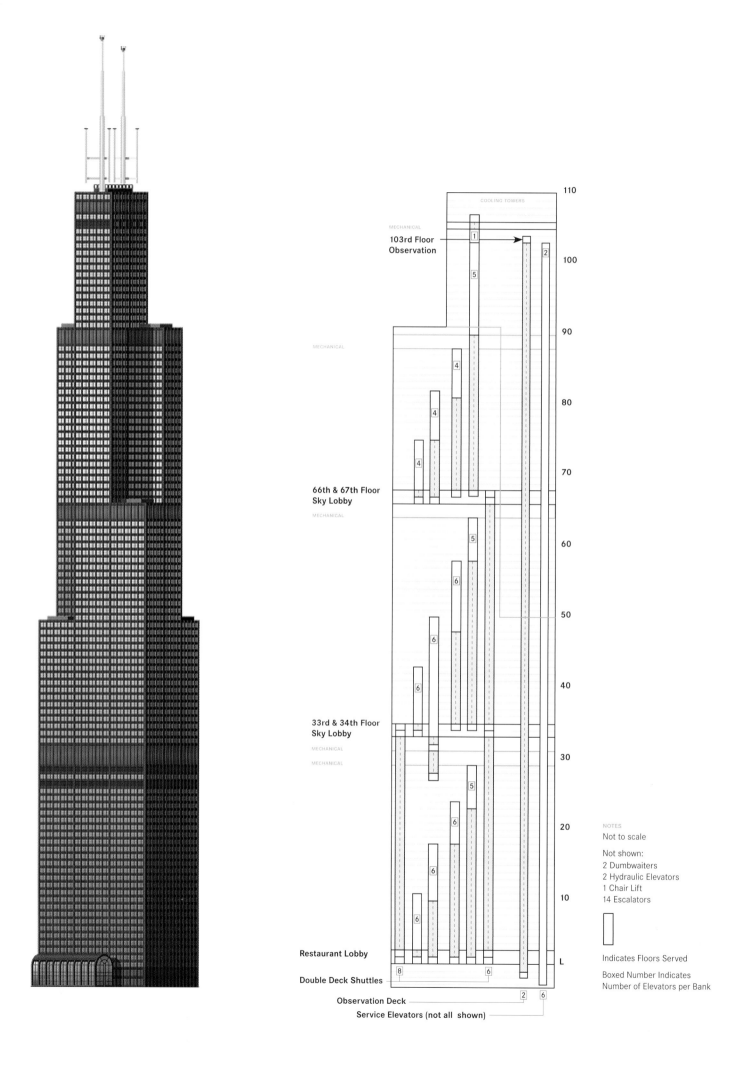

110

COOLING TOWERS

MECHANICAL

103rd Floor
Observation

100

90

MECHANICAL

80

70

66th & 67th Floor
Sky Lobby

MECHANICAL

60

50

40

33rd & 34th Floor
Sky Lobby

MECHANICAL

MECHANICAL

30

20

10

Restaurant Lobby

L

Double Deck Shuttles

Observation Deck

Service Elevators (not all shown)

NOTES

Not to scale

Not shown:
2 Dumbwaiters
2 Hydraulic Elevators
1 Chair Lift
14 Escalators

Indicates Floors Served

Boxed Number Indicates
Number of Elevators per Bank

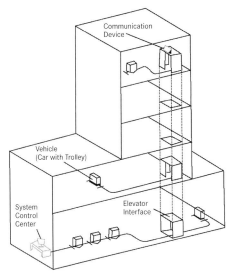

115 TOP
FROG Park Shuttle, 1998, part of the Schiphol Project, Amsterdam Airport, The Netherlands.

116 CENTER
SchindlerMobile®, 1997.

117 ABOVE
Automated Guided Vehicle Riser Diagram, c. 1990.

This diagram shows how self-propelled automatic guided vehicles can move about in a building between a wide variety of stations, and even between floors.

118 OPPOSITE LEFT
Drawing of Sears Tower, Chicago, designed by Skidmore, Owings & Merrill, 1974.

119 OPPOSITE RIGHT
Sears Tower elevator diagram, 2003. Drawing by Richard Evans.

elevated park in a regional garden exposition [115].[18] An underground logistics system planned for Schiphol proposes to connect the airport to the Flower Auction at Aalsmeer, logistics centers in the surrounding area, and a rail terminal. Hundreds of AGVs would transfer materials along a bi-directional tunnel.[19] Such logistical tunnels handling baggage and air cargo are emerging as the automated infrastructures of competitive global hubs. Many cities have considered building a large-scale underground logistics network to serve an entire city, or a utility system that delivers storage and freight, rather than water and gas. In a description of his design for the extension of New York's Museum of Modern Art, the Dutch architect Rem Koolhaas writes:

"There are two areas in which recent inventions can make a radical difference, control and transport. . . . Robotics replace laborious, unwieldy processes of storage, retrieval, sorting, and reshuffling with smooth movements of frenzied ease that force us to rethink entire systems of classification and categorization. . . . The second innovation is in transport. As more and more architecture is finally unmasked as the mere organization of flow—shopping centers, airports—it is evident that circulation is what makes or breaks public architecture. . . . Two simple, almost primitive, inventions have driven modernization toward mass occupancy of previously unattainable heights: the elevator and the escalator. . . . One moves only up and down, one only diagonally. . . .

At the dawn of the 21st century, a number of advances in vertical transportation are being made, from cableless self-propelled elevator systems to Otis' . . . Odyssey, a small train, platform, or large box that moves horizontally, vertically, and diagonally—literally opening up new architectural potential: to extend the urban condition itself from the ground floor to strategic points inside a building in a continuous trajectory."[20]

Several companies are further narrowing the distance between cars, logistics conveyance, and personal transport by making the elevator into a device that can leave the shaft or operate in multiples within the shaft. The SchindlerMobile, now called the SchindlerEurolift, was the result of a collaboration with Porsche to build what was called the "slowest Porsche on Earth."[21] It moves horizontally through a building and then, when linked with a sister mechanism, acquires the traction necessary for moving vertically [116]. The Otis project mentioned by Koolhaas, the Odyssey system, has projected an elevator so adaptable that it could move horizontally through a parking lot and then vertically or horizontally through a building along a guide track, requiring no hoist or machine room. Since the shaft is designed to handle more than one cab, Otis claimed that height restrictions based on volume of traffic or number of floors could be lifted to make way for taller towers. Otis had already marketed the product to skyscrapers planned for China, Indonesia, Hong Kong, Korea, and Singapore, but discontinued promotion of the project after the attack on the World Trade Center in September 2001. Many of the proposals for rebuilding the World Trade Center site, though perhaps not as spatially complex as their systems of elevatoring, have included circulation systems with both vertical and horizontal movement. These were not necessarily used as the means to greater height, but as the means to a more resilient networked organization of circulation that would replace the World Trade Center's slow, sequential means of escape.

The history of a company called Translogic/Swisslog illustrates the larger story of the rapprochement between the car and the conveyance device. Originally based in the automobile capital of Detroit, the company at one time manufactured pneumatic tube systems. After merging with Swisslog, however, it became a global leader in supply-chain mechanisms of all kinds—pneumatics, electric track vehicles, AGVs, vertical conveyors, and mail-sorting machines.

120 ABOVE
The Intelligent Transcar Automated Guided Vehicle,
c. 1990.

121 OPPOSITE
Aerial intermodal yard and airport, Alliance, Texas, 2002.

Translogic makes a battery-operated, infrared-controlled AGV called the Transcar that is marketed to hospitals, universities, and mail centers [120]. Transcars move back and forth between, for instance, a laundry and a lab, via logistical levels and tunnels. By combining automobile and conveyance functions, the Transcar is able to call an elevator, select a floor, and exit on that floor by means of infrared signals from the controlling computer.[22]

While dreams of liberation accompany visions of automated omnidirectional conveyance, conveyance germs also help to shape the political arena. As an element in the cultural scripts variously associated with industry, warfare, or science fiction, these devices are projected to reduce friction and operate logically according to the new organizational paradigms. It is possible for buildings to be taller, traffic jams reduced, and, in the new logistics city, the movement of goods to be optimized in urban formations that avoid political and legal constraints. Yet, at the same moment that tall buildings have become the part of the apparatus of warfare, these "duty-free" special economic zones, in their association with each other, have begun to establish new cross-national political entities that may begin to play a much more complex and less predictable political game. The conveyance germ is not the obedient component of an urban master plan, but an opportunistic agent that generates a political complexity beyond the control of urban planning.

The elevator informed the development of the tall building, not only as an architectural endeavor but also as a real-estate formula that generated the global financial city [118, 119]. The automobile similarly shaped a highway network and a spreading suburban landscape. The new hybrids of the two vehicles, each occasionally adopting the repertoire of the other, are generating a new type of global city, but they may also land opportunistically in earlier urban formations, looking for an economic or temporary technological imperative. Controlled by infrared, laser, radio, transponder, or even GPS, these hybrid vehicles suggest that the construction of space comes to resemble the construction of the open field of broadcast of which they are part. Although never without friction, as conveyance germs adopt ever larger and more complex terrains as navigable surfaces, they have the potential to defamiliarize our most familiar modes of enclosure and urbanism.

1. Miriam Lacob, "Elevators on the Move," *Scientific American*, October 1997.

2. http://www.otis.com/aboutotis/companyinfo/0,1360, CLI1_RES1,00.html
Among the first Otis appearances were the Crystal Palace exhibition in New York City in 1853 and the Eiffel Tower in 1888. Even the company's earliest and most prominent tall building commissions, the Flatiron Building in 1902 and the Woolworth Building in 1912, celebrated the delirium of stacked environments and monumental profiles.

3. Narration from a film accompanying the Futurama exhibition, *To New Horizons*, General Motors, 1939. http://barbra-public.alexa.com:8080/ramgen/net/movie1/0/pub/movies/reallb/07906.rm.

4. Ibid.

5. Bruno Latour, *Aramis or The Love of Technology* [1992], trans. Catherine Porter, Cambridge, Massachusetts (Harvard University Press) 1996.

6. http://www.otis.com/aboutotis/companyinfo/0,1360, CLI1_RES1,00.html
As of 1925, and the installation of an elevator with "memory" in a Chicago hospital, elevators were already automated. Elevators continue to develop intelligence, diagnosing their own operating defects and developing behaviors to respond to changing conditions and needs.

7. The Interstate Highway System was created by Congress with the passage of the Federal-Aid Highway Act of 1956.

8. "AGVs: A bigger hit in other places – by far," *Modern Materials Handling*, Boston, April 1996, vol. 51, iss. 4, 13; http://www.frog.nl/eng/industry/situation/index.html.

9. *The Washington Times*, October 3, 2002.

10. http://www.frog.nl/eng/cargo/situation/index.html.

11. http://www.eaglehawksc.vic.edu.au/kla/technology/robots/autodock/article.htm.

12. R.H. Hollier and L.F. Gelders, eds., "Automated Handling of Intermodal Containers with AGVs: Automated Guided Vehicle Systems," *Proceedings of the 6th International Conference*, 1988, pp. 287–325.

13. Les Gould, "Free-Ranging AGVs Cover 100,000-sq-ft Assembly Area," *Modern Materials Handling*, Boston, December 14, 1994, vol. 49, iss. 14, pp. 46–48.

14. Ir. C. Versteegt and Prof. Dr H.G. Sol, "The design of logistic control for intermodal transport chains of the 21st century," TRAIL Research School, Delft, December, 1999, p. 14.

15. "Hong Kong as the world's leading port: a concept paper on e-commerce and logistics," December 1999, http://www.hkcsi.org.hk/papers/submit/9912ecomm.htm.

16. Ibid.

17. http://www.psa.com.sg/.

18. http://www.frog.nl/eng/peoplemovers/solution/solution.html; and http://faculty.washington.edu/jbs/itrans/parkshut.htm.

19. A. Verbraeck and C. Versteegt, "Logistical Control for Fully Automated Large-Scale Freight Transport Systems," 2000. http://216.239.51.100/search?q=cache:APTZzOxExK0C:cttrailf.ct.tudelft.nl/ftam/papers/verbraeck_versteegt_ieee.pdf+automated+logistics+tunnel&hl=en&ie=UTF-8.

20. http://www.moma.org/expansion/charette/architects/koolhaas.

21. M. Lacob, "Elevators on the Move," *Scientific American*, October 1997; http://www.schindler.com/man/webnews2.nsf/Web/Corporate-010116e.

22. When J.C. Penney moved its mail facility from Manhattan to Plano, Texas, it deployed a fleet of Transcar vehicles of different types that moved through the building delivering mail, alerting employees of its arrival with a "friendly chime." http://www.translogic-corp.com/jcpenney_apps.htm.

Perspectives on the Escalator
in Photography and Art

Julie Wosk

122
**Otis Escalator at the Paris Exposition Universelle,
1900.**

At the dawn of a new century, a photograph taken at the Paris Exposition in 1900 captured an exciting new form of transportation: an electrically-driven moving staircase [122]. The escalator, with its oak treads and balustrades fitted with plate-glass panels, was designed by American engineer Charles Seeberger and manufactured by the Otis Elevator Company out of their Yonkers, New York facility. It was used to transport visitors to America's exhibit in the Textile Section, and won the exposition's Grand Prix.[1]

In the photograph, the escalator looms dramatically, framed by the company's large cast-iron entrance with its classical Ionic columns and the word "Escalator" displayed on the lintel overhead. In ancient Greece, propylaea were architectural gateways that ushered people into the precincts of structures such as the Parthenon on the Acropolis in Athens, but at the 1900 Exposition in Paris, Otis's imposing cast-iron frame became a portal ushering visitors into a new world of technological progress and fast-moving machines.

The nineteenth century had long been fascinated with technological speed and efficiency and, by the 1890s, not only steam railroads and electric elevated railway systems, but also newly invented steam, electric, and gasoline automobiles were offering new and efficient forms of transportation. For many, this burst of technological inventiveness brought a heady sense of exhilaration,

yet there were some concerns, too, about these new technologies speeding out of control.[2]

Nineteenth-century American and European manufacturers had already produced designs for stationary steam engines with neoclassical cast-iron frames. Railroad stations were also designed with neoclassical motifs, as seen in London's Euston Station, built in the 1830s with its classical temple-like façade, and this trend later reappeared in the neoclassicism of stations such as McKim, Mead, and White's Pennsylvania Station in New York (1906–10).[3]

These neoclassical frameworks helped introduce new technologies and to dignify them, giving them an air of grandeur and prestige. In the nineteenth century's age of steam, they also helped create an atmosphere of stasis and order, as people were about to travel on the new, potentially explosive railroad engines. At the Paris Exposition of 1900, the experience of stepping on to a relatively slow-moving staircase would have been much less disconcerting, but still unfamiliar to many visitors. Otis's columned, neoclassical entrance not only lent grandeur to the machine but also created an aura of familiarity and calm.

In 1898, before working with Otis on the Paris escalator design, Seeberger had taken over inventor George Wheeler's patents for a step-type escalator. With their flat, ridged steps, Otis's early escalator designs made it easy for people to stand but required waist-high shunts at the landings to guide passengers off to the side in order to exit safely. (The word "Escalator" itself, so boldly planted over the Seeberger escalator in Paris, had been coined by Seeberger, who registered it with a capital "E" as a trademarked name. Otis bought out Seeberger in 1910, and the company held the Escalator trademark until 1950 when a court ruled that the word had become generic and was in the public domain.)

In 1892, Seeberger's chief competitor, engineer Jesse Reno, had already patented his own designs for an "inclined elevator," a type of upward-tilting conveyer belt with cleats rather than steps and grooved landings which made it easier for riders to step on and off. (In 1911, Otis bought out Reno's patents, and by the 1920s the company had combined the best of both Reno's and Seeberger's designs, creating a step-type escalator with grooved landings.)[4]

While the highly symmetrical Paris photograph framed the machine in formality and calm, a painting of an amusement park ride at Coney Island associated the escalator with excitement and thrills [123]. In 1892, Reno had begun experimenting with inclined, cleat-type escalators at the Brooklyn Bridge, and in September 1896 a Reno escalator was used to transport 75,000 people at Coney Island up a 7-foot (2-meter) incline to the old iron pier.[5] During the 1906–07 season, an escalator was also used to transport people up to the ride called Helter-Skelter at Coney Island's newest attraction, Luna Park [125].[6]

Opened in 1903, Luna Park was a huge and spectacular amusement park illuminated at night by a dazzling display of electric lights. The park featured thirty-one buildings and twenty-eight rides, including Helter-Skelter, a ride introduced by Frederic Thompson, one of the park's developers, as a chute 50 feet (15 meters) long that was reached by riding up an inclined escalator. If the cast-iron entrance to Otis's Paris escalator evoked an image of stability and dignity, Helter-Skelter—as the ride's name implied—conjured up the look and feel of joyous abandon and visceral down-to-earth fun. Riders sat on a high-sided rattan slide that took a twisting and turning route, landing people on a mattress on the ground with attendants standing nearby. In 1906 the slide was improved to include two chutes that started out side-by-side but then split up and rejoined at the bottom, offering couples the possibility of a romantic ride [124].

By the end of the nineteenth century, engineers also recognized the value of escalators in moving large numbers of people through urban rapid-transit systems. The inclined escalator used by Jesse Reno in 1896 at Coney Island was tested a

123 ABOVE
Helter-Skelter and escalator at Luna Park, Coney Island, New York, 1902.

124 OPPOSITE
Postcard of the Helter-Skelter slide at Luna Park, Coney Island, New York, 1905.

125 Postcard of "The Scaler," Luna Park, Coney Island, New York, *c.* 1905.

THE SCALER, LUNA PARK, CONEY ISLAND, N.Y.

SCI.AM.N.Y.

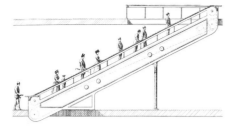

126 TOP
A Reno experimental escalator at the Brooklyn Bridge, New York, 1892.

127 ABOVE
The Seeberger escalator at the 23rd Street Elevated Railroad Station, New York, *c.* **1903.**

128 OPPOSITE
A Reno "inclined elevator" at the Brooklyn Bridge, New York, 1897. From *Scientific American,* January 16, 1897.

year later to transport people up to the Brooklyn elevated railroad platform on the New York side of the Brooklyn Bridge.

Reno had been experimenting with escalators in Brooklyn since 1892, and his design patented that year was intended not only for urban elevated railroad systems but also for retail stores and railroad stations. His design—which the American journal *Engineering News* called a "continuous elevator"—moved passengers along an inclined belt pitched at a twenty-five-degree angle, moving at 100 feet (30.5 meters) per minute.[7] Given the escalator's narrow width, passengers rode single file, spaced 18 inches (45.7 cm) apart, as seen in an illustration supplied by Reno to the *News* [126].

By 1897, magazines such as *Scientific American* were publishing illustrations suggesting that people were becoming acclimatized to the new machine, one example being an artist's view of Reno's Brooklyn Bridge escalator, which traveled on an incline of 7 feet (2 meters) beside a bridge stairway and moved at 80 feet (24 meters) per minute [128].[8] By 1900, the 59th Street Station of the Third Avenue El had Reno-type inclined escalators (which remained in operation until the line was torn down in 1955). The Manhattan Elevated Railroad ordered 100 Reno-type inclined elevators the same year, and a Seeberger escalator was installed at the 23rd Street Station of New York Elevated Railroad's Sixth Avenue Line.[9] In 1904, Seeberger himself wrote a story about escalators, which was published in the American engineering magazine *Cassier's*. It included an artist's rendering of people traveling on the escalator [127].

In his story, which also included photographs of the newly installed escalators at Macy's, Seeberger emphasized the escalator's safety. "The first essential of design," he wrote, "is to inspire confidence on the part of the passenger," which, he added, made his step design particularly reassuring since it was "an architectural feature familiar to all from infancy" and associated with safety. Escalator riders, he noted, could travel with "the same certainty as upon a stationary stairway, for its motion does not affect equilibrium."[10]

The illustration for Seeberger's story focuses on a young girl and her mother riding up to the station platform. The little girl stands tall on the escalator's steps without holding her mother's hand or the handrail, creating the image of an easy ride. The casually chatting riders in the story's illustration also seem to reinforce Seeberger's point.

The escalator's association with speed and efficiency led architects in England to perceive it as the perfect vehicle for transferring passengers from one tube line to another in London's vast underground railroad network. In 1900, the British journal *Engineering* featured an illustration of a curving escalator, a "proposed circular escalation" at the Paris Exposition, and in 1906 it published a drawing of a spiral design intended for the London underground—a "double spiral continuous moving track" or type of double-helix escalator designed by Jesse Reno's Reno Electric Stairways and Conveyers Company.

Reno's spiral design was intended for the Holloway Road station of the London Underground's new Great North, Piccadilly, and Brompton line. The spiral escalator allowed passengers to travel in both directions, had a rise of 35 feet (11 meters), and moved at 100 feet (30.5 meters) per minute. It was installed on an experimental basis, and there is no evidence that it ever entered passenger service.[11] Seeberger, meanwhile, was developing his own spiral design for the London Underground, seen in his artfully drawn illustration, but the escalator was never actually built [129].

In 1911 the *Illustrated London News* reported that London had finally "come in line with New York" by installing the first escalators in its underground rapid transit system. The Otis Elevator Company made two adjoining escalators, one going up, and one going down, for Earl's Court Station.[12] Dubbing them "London's New

ESCALATOR
CONVEYING PASSENGERS IN EITHER DIRECTION
FOR
UNDERGROUND ROAD.
Designed and Patented by
CHARLES D. SEEBERGER.

129 Seeberger's spiral escalator design for the London Underground, 1911.

130 OPPOSITE Details of Seeberger's escalator at Earl's Court Underground Station, London, 1911. From *Illustrated London News*, October 14, 1911.

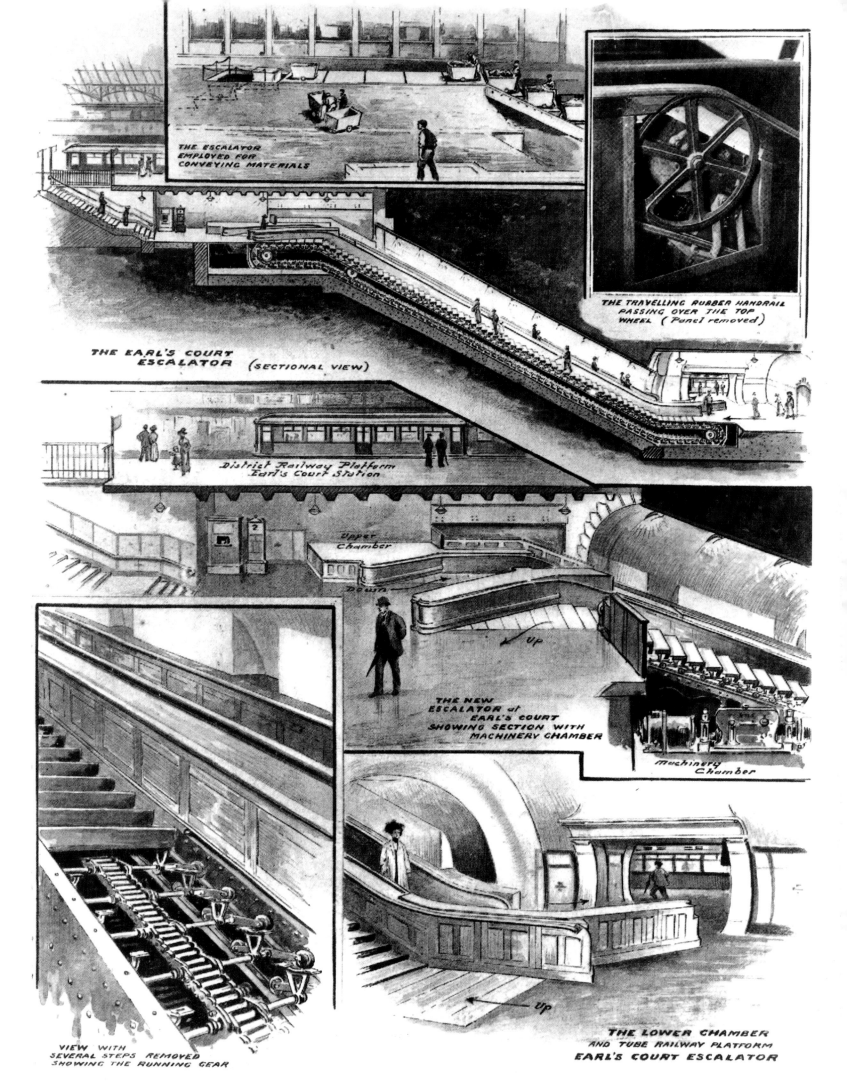

THE ESCALATOR EMPLOYED FOR CONVEYING MATERIALS

THE TRAVELLING RUBBER HANDRAIL PASSING OVER THE TOP WHEEL (Panel removed)

THE EARL'S COURT ESCALATOR (SECTIONAL VIEW)

District Railway Platform Earl's Court Station

Upper Chamber

Down

Up

THE NEW ESCALATOR at EARL'S COURT SHOWING SECTION WITH MACHINERY CHAMBER

Machinery Chamber

VIEW WITH SEVERAL STEPS REMOVED SHOWING THE RUNNING GEAR

Up

THE LOWER CHAMBER AND TUBE RAILWAY PLATFORM EARL'S COURT ESCALATOR

THE TOP OF THE STAIRWAY.

UNDERGROUND
PLEASE DO NOT SIT
ON THE STAIRS

STEP OFF WITH
LEFT FOOT FIRST

Amusement," the newspaper included a full-page engraving of a painting by illustrator S. Begg depicting Londoners ascending and descending en route between the Piccadilly line and the District Railway at the station [132]. Begg's illustration presented an array of escalator travelers, suggesting the broad cross-section of people who converged in the underground system.

In the story, the escalator is portrayed as a boon to travel and a novelty for passengers and readers alike. For escalator riders at Earl's Court Station, "Pleasure is combined with business," and some people were even so fascinated by the machine that they have "traveled up, then down, then up again before their curiosity and desire for a new sensation have been satisfied." As was appropriate for a new technology, the newspaper also detailed for its readers just how the machine operated (passengers entered on a horizontal platform traveling 90 feet (27 meters) per minute, the platform gradually became stairs, and then returned to a platform again as the travelers exited), and included a photograph of the handrail passing over a wheel and sectional views of the machinery [130].[13]

For all of the pleasure and fascination in escalator riding, however, Begg's illustration was also a reminder that the machine was still unfamiliar and had the potential for mishaps. On the divider between the handrails, the artist has included the signs, "Please do not sit on the stairs" and "Step off with left foot first."[14]

In an early photograph of escalators being used in a large industrial building, workers at the Wood Worsted Mill in Lawrence, Massachusetts, are pictured riding in crowded but orderly rows [131]. The Wood Mill, which was the first factory to utilize escalators, ordered four from Seeberger in 1905, and more a few years later. The company's escalators carried their 6300 workers for short periods during the day: up in the morning, down and up at noon, and down at night, between the second and sixth floors.[15] In a later advertising booklet, published in 1928, Otis described these escalators as a "time-and-money saver," conserving the energy and time of workers. Promoting the machines, Otis again took a sanguine view, seeing them as reflecting industrial benevolence, for they helped employers get "the most expert" workers who were "attracted to a plant where their welfare and health are conscientiously considered."[16]

This same view had appeared earlier when Otis extolled the use of escalators in department stores. In *Moving Your Customers and What They Buy* (1915), the company featured photographs of employees' escalators at an Abraham & Straus Department Store in Brooklyn. By using the escalators, workers avoided climbing two flights of stairs, and there was another pay off: the "refreshed and cheerful attitude of employees and their greater capacity for work."[17]

The benefits of using escalators in department stores had been recognized years earlier. At the end of the nineteenth century in cities like New York, Paris, and London, newly built multi-storied department stores and 5- and 10-cent stores became emblems of new, modern, and efficient ways to market a large quantity of goods. Storeowners sought ways to move customers more quickly to upper floors, increase their sales, and efficiently display their wares.

Early stories in engineering, architectural, and popular magazines enthused about the escalator's benefits in department stores: escalators moved large numbers of people at a uniform rate, and carried them continuously rather than having them queue up to wait for an elevator ride; unlike elevators, escalators didn't require attendants; they conserved energy and promoted customer circulation in the stores; and they gave customers a panoramic, birds-eye view of sales items throughout the store—increasing the possibility of impulse buying. Escalators, *Architects' and Builders' Magazine* (1912) concluded, helped make the upper

131 ABOVE
Workers at Wood Worsted Mill, Lawrence, Massachusetts, c. 1910.

132 OPPOSITE
Escalator at Earl's Court Underground Station, London, 1911. From *Illustrated London News*, October 14, 1911.

stories as accessible as the first, which "would work a wonderful revolution in department stores."[18]

As early as 1896, Jesse Reno had sold four belt-type escalators to Siegel Cooper Department Store in Manhattan and in 1898 *The Electrical Engineer* wrote excitedly about the installation of an "inclined elevator" built by Reno for travel between the first and second floors at Bloomingdale Brothers Department Store, located in Manhattan between 59th and 60th Streets on Third Avenue. The Reno escalator, three-and-a-half foot (one meter) wide, was intended for single-file service, and was built at an angle of about twenty-five degrees. Again, the journal told readers about the ride: passengers stood on rubber-covered wooden ridges or slats and held on to a moving handrail (covered with white disks so that passengers knew it was moving). At the end of the ride, customers walked off as they approached the comb-shaped landing.

The store escalator, according to the journal, had already moved more than 50,000 customers while relieving them of fatigue and, unlike the elevator, the escalator ran "free from shocks and jars." The journal also reassured readers that not a single accident had occurred and that the escalators could be stopped and started by pushing a button. The ride could even be considered liberating for the claustrophobic, because "the sensations of the passengers are apparently more agreeable than when shut up in the closed cage of an ordinary elevator." Summing up the machine's advantages, the journal wrote euphorically that the escalator was "one of the greatest conveniences yet devised for the comfortable handling of large masses of people circulating indoors."[19]

Bloomingdale's six-story building had already seen the addition of elegant elevators fitted with plate-glass mirrors, fine mahogany, and upholstered seats, but it was the escalator that was considered a great attention-grabber in the city.[20] *The Electrical Engineer* story included a side view of people riding single file up the escalator and a more dramatic and closely cropped image of a solitary woman ascending the inclined escalator [133]. Seen only from the back, without her face in view, the woman here becomes a generic female shopper, an anonymous model demonstrating the new machine. She leans to the right as she holds on to the handrail, a reminder of the somewhat awkward incline. Her long skirt, meanwhile, becomes a reminder of the designers' needs to avoid clothing mishaps at the landing point (the journal is upbeat, noting that "the landing is a most agreeable and natural one"; indeed, it is "so perfect . . . that even cotton waste will not catch at this point").[21]

Creating a visual counterpoint, a group of formally dressed men stand nearby, not watching the woman on the escalator but gazing into the camera instead, registering their identities and presence at this important demonstration of a new machine.

Step escalators, such as that designed by Seeberger, allowed up to three people to stand on one of the step landings. In 1900, a Seeberger-type escalator built by Otis was installed in a Simpson, Crawford & Simpson department store in Manhattan and in 1901, Seeberger's step-type escalator used at the Paris Exposition was sold to Gimbel Brothers Department Store in Philadelphia (the escalator remained in operation until 1939 when it was replaced by more up-to-date Otis equipment).[22] By 1902, Macy's Department Store in New York could boast of being the first department store to have escalators beyond the second floor, having installed the first bank of four Seeberger escalators traveling from the first up to the fifth floor, and in 1903, a Boston department store became the first one to have up and down escalators.[23]

One of the biggest advantages of department store escalators—according to early advertisers—was that they allowed masses of people to ascend in a continuous fashion, moving many more people than could be accommodated in an

133
Woman riding a Reno escalator, 1898. From *Electrical Engineering*, July 7, 1898.

134 Illustration showing a typical installation of the cleat-step type escalator, 1929.

135 OPPOSITE An "electric travelling stairway" in a department store, *c.* 1904. From Edwin J. Houston, *Electricity in Every-Day Life*, *Vol. II*, New York (P.P. Collier & Son) 1905.

elevator. Early photos of passengers, though, gave opposing views of the experience. Photographs of Reno escalators, like the one at Bloomingdale's, show people riding single file, conveying a sense of order and calm, but images of people standing on the wider steps of the Seeberger escalators sometimes presented views of teeming groups of department store shoppers jammed together in almost overflow capacity. In a photograph in Edwin J. Houston's three-volume *Electricity in Every-Day Life* (1905), a large group of female shoppers with beaming faces look almost comically crowded on the steps of an "electric traveling stairway" in a department store [135].[24] These crowded images may have been meant to highlight the advantages of escalators and the great number of people they could transport.

Escalators, according to the manufacturers, were not only a wonderfully efficient way to move customers but also offered them a whole new way of seeing—presenting them with dramatic, panoramic, and unfolding views. Escalator riders not only saw merchandise at a distance, but also slices of space—shards of a view shaped by the diagonal lines of escalator balustrades.

In its early booklet on escalators for 5- and 10-cent stores, Otis included a compressed photographic view of customers traveling on a duplex escalator in a Woolworth's store in Newark, New Jersey, gazing at the great piles of merchandise on floors above and below [138]. The photo, like so many images of escalators, had its own type of technological dynamism: multiple vanishing points, the sharply receding diagonals of the escalators and the spaces that they defined.[25]

By 1922, Otis was working to lend its escalators an international and even a glamorous appeal. Its 1922 advertising booklet featured an artist's illustration of customers at the Mitsukoshi Department Store in Japan, showing women customers wearing traditional kimonos but still availing themselves of this modern technology [136].[26] A 1928 booklet featured an artist's drawings of fashionable men and women shoppers, presenting the scene—and the escalators—with 1920s elegance [134].

In the early part of the twentieth century, the Italian and Russian futurist artists wrote ecstatically about modern speed and technology. They relished the idea of speeding automobiles and trains, seeing in them the spirit of a radically new age. Writing in their manifesto of 1910, the Italian futurists called for a sweeping aside of old subjects of art in favor of images of new technologies: "all subjects previously used must be swept aside to express our whirling life of steel, of pride, or fever, of headlong speed."[27]

By the 1930s, the aerodynamic shapes of airplanes had inspired a new aesthetic, one echoing the tapered, wind-swept shapes of the DC-1, 2, and 3. In industrial design, adulation of airplane speed and styling became a hallmark of streamlining, or what was then called the Streamlined Moderne.[28] Streamlining, Sheldon Cheney wrote in *Art and the Machine* (1936), had become a symbol "borrowed from airplanes and made to compel the eye anew."[29]

During the 1930s Otis produced its own streamlined designs and, in a 1936 advertisement for the Otis Streamlined Escalator, the company featured an escalator designed by New York interior designer Eleanor LeMaire (and her staff) for the San Francisco department store The Emporium [137]. In her design LeMaire, who went on to become one of the few women specializing in business interiors in the 1960s, worked toward creating a shopping atmosphere filled with glamour and theatricality. The image portrays a group of well-dressed shoppers riding on an escalator made glamorous with sand-blasted glass (illuminated from within), tinted coral, and accents of nickel-bronze metal.

The ad included a small inset photograph of LeMaire's face, thereby linking the escalator's streamlined design not only to department store shopping, but to

136 TOP
Mitsukoshi Department Store, Tokyo, c. 1922.

137 ABOVE
Advertisement for Otis Elevator Company Streamlined Escalators, c. 1936.

138 OPPOSITE
Escalator at a Woolworth's Store, Newark, New Jersey, c. 1900.

EADY NOW FOR THE WORLD OF TOMORROW

1939

THE MACHINE AND CAB WHICH YOU SEE HERE
REPRESENT THE LATEST DESIGNS IN ELEVATOR
EQUIPMENT. THE ELEVATORS WHICH WILL
SERVE THE WORLD OF TOMORROW ARE BE-
ING PERFECTED BY OTIS ENGINEERS TODAY.

THE OTIS SIGNAL CONTROL ELECTRIC ELEVATOR
WHETHER USED WITH FINGER-TIP CONTROL
PROVIDES THE HIGHEST CLASS OF ELEVATOR SERVICE.

ESCALATORS
"the modern magic carpet"

THE FIRST ESCALATOR WAS INTRODUCED TO THE PUBLIC BY OTIS AT THE PARIS EXPO

OTIS

139 TOP
Advertisement for the Otis Elevator Company's "Free-Flow" Escalators, 1955.

140 ABOVE
Advertisement for the Otis Elevator Company's "Esca-Laire," c. 1963.

141 OPPOSITE
Otis Elevator Company exhibit at the World's Fair, New York, 1939.

femininity—emphasizing that the escalator lent itself to "a woman's touch." LeMaire's design was "in harmony with a woman's world," and not just a quotidian form of transport but the very essence of modernity: "Escalators," LeMaire is quoted as saying, "are an integral part of our modern age and they cannot be ignored."

In 1939 – 40, New York City played host to the World's Fair and its hallmark presentation of the World of Tomorrow. In Flushing, Queens, the towering geometries of the Trylon, 70 feet (21 meters) high, and the dome of the Perisphere summed up the country's pride in its machine-age technologies and its optimistic hopes for the future. The Otis Company's exhibit situated its escalators and elevators in the world of fast-moving, streamlined transportation machines.

Located in the Hall of Industry, Metals Building, Otis's exhibit room included a large, gearless elevator motor and a mock elevator complete with a male mannequin dressed as a uniformed elevator operator. There were also two large posters on the wall celebrating transportation machines [141]. Otis, one poster proclaimed, was "READY NOW for the world of tomorrow," and it featured the tapered bodies of a railroad locomotive, an automobile, a ship, and a bus. A second huge poster advertised escalators as "the modern magic carpet," and pictured a V-shaped view of a woman in a business suit riding on one of the company's streamlined escalator designs, its balustrade ornamented with metallic lines. Behind her is an image of criss-crossed abstracted escalators with silhouettes of passengers. Here is a woman, the poster suggests, taking a magic ride to a modern new realm.

In the period following World War II, Otis advertising featured contrasting images: in an advertisement from 1955, women shoppers on an Otis "Free-Flow" escalator wear sensible coats and point with exaggerated, open-mouthed excitement at items in the store, while later escalator images are infused with glamour and style [139].

The company lost its copyright claim to the capitalized word "Escalator" in 1950, and in 1962 it trademarked the name "Esca-Laire" for a line of escalators with glass balustrades; these were marketed for shopping centers and the lobbies of office buildings and hotels. During the 1960s, Esca-Laire ads featured artists' images of men in tuxedos and women in furs lounging near the glass balustrades of lobby escalators [140]. Here was a different type of magical world, complete with stars and a crescent moon. Readers were asked to visualize balustrades that were "crystal clear," "sparkling," "light and airy," and "intriguingly translucent," with handrail colors "picked from a rainbow." With their see-through balustrades, the Esca-Laire escalators mirrored their patrons' best conceptions of themselves: the machines had a quiet glamour without ostentation but could be "boldly scintillating."

While manufacturers and advertisers were creating images of escalators endowed with glamour and style, a small number of American painters and photographers created their own escalator images, recasting them anew. At the beginning of the twentieth century, Italian futurist and Russian Cubo-futurist artists celebrated a world of electricity and new transportation machines. Absorbing aspects of both Cubism and futurism, American painter Joseph Stella created iconic images of the Brooklyn Bridge, and his painting *Battle of Lights: Coney Island* (1914) presented a frenzied view of the whirling amusement park rides at night. Decades later, in the 1940s, New Jersey artist Mari-Louise Van Esselstyn drew on Cubist idioms as she revealed her own fascination with movement, the escalator, and transportation machines.

Using small brushes and egg tempera on gessoed panels, the artist created carefully crafted images of moving machines such as *The Mole* (1947) and her views of the New Haven railroad and the Roundabout, an amusement-park ride.

159

Perspectives on the Escalator

In her energized painting *The Escalator* (1943–44), she presented the frenetic activity of travelers through her use of Cubist-inspired fragmented forms and overlapping planes [143].

In a handwritten comment, Van Esselstyn noted that as a painter she was trying to reproduce the look of motion in the exacting medium of egg tempera, and *The Escalator* is indeed a paradoxical blend of precision and movement.[30] Her painting presents a sharply faceted view of people hurrying through a small city bus terminal, perhaps the station of Montclair, New Jersey, from which she left to take buses to New York and then on to New Haven, Connecticut, when she attended the Yale School of Art.[31]

Van Esselstyn stated that she wanted to "create the illusion of movement," and in *The Escalator* she achieves this in a variety of ways: the rectangular patterning of escalator steps; the Cubist interplay of abstracted figures of people moving in opposite directions, like the silhouetted figure of a woman striding to the right; and the long, diagonal slashes of light streaming from the station windows on the upper left.

While Van Esselstyn's painting embedded the escalator into the hurried activity of a busy bus station, the machine and its riders take center stage in Marjorie Collins's photograph taken at New York's Pennsylvania Railroad Station during the war years of the 1940s [142]. Collins was one of a group of American photographers—and only a small number of women—who were hired by the American government to take documentary photographs for the Farm Security Administration (FSA), an agency that was superseded by the Office of War Information in 1942.[32] Escalators had become essential to the moving of people at Penn Station since the first Seeberger escalators were installed there in 1909, and in her photograph Collins captures the crowds of people, including the delighted faces of children riding on the machine.

Nearly 30 years later, in his two paintings of escalators done in 1970 and 1971, both simply titled *Escalator*, American photorealist artist Richard Estes made the machines themselves the primary subject. There are no passengers in these paintings, just close-up views of curving balustrades and gleaming metallic surfaces. In *Escalator* (1970), Estes crops the image into the first few steps so that the entry point yawns wide, inviting us to step aboard [144]. The curving sides of the balustrade seem to offer the fun of swooping down on a ride.

But Estes's escalator also offers another view: the dancing, abstracted patterns of light and shadow reflected in the shiny, mirrored metal of the balustrades. With their muted grays and yellows, the reflections become miniature paintings in their own right—creating a dramatic interplay of flat geometries and a counterpoint to the escalator's curvilinear sides.

Estes's escalator paintings continued the modernist and precisionist painters' preoccupation with seeing abstraction in the forms of machines. In the first decades of the twentieth century, painters such as Philadelphia-born Morton Livingston Schamberg were among the first to focus on the clean lines, spare geometries, and classic simplicity of machines, and Schamberg's *Mechanical Abstraction* (1916) endowed machine parts with dignity and a fluid grace. In the 1920s and 1930s, America's precisionist painters, including Charles Sheeler, created images of machines as classically spare and pristine. In his painting *Ballet Mechanique* (1931), Sheeler created an elegant distillation of the rhythmic, curving pipes at Ford's River Rouge Plant near Detroit. In Sheeler's paintings, all is clarity and order, devoid of any people who might distract from the machines.

From 1966–69, Estes had painted cropped, fragmented images of automobile windshields, rear windows, hoods, and chrome. Commenting about these paintings, Estes said, "My idea was to do realism but be abstract at the same time."[33] Extending the focus of the precisionists, Estes added a fascination with surface

142 ABOVE
Escalators at Pennsylvania Railroad Station, New York, 1942.

143 OPPOSITE
Mari-Louise Van Esselstyn, *The Escalator*, 1942.

144 **Richard Estes**, *Escalator*, 1970.

reflections and sheen: his paintings often captured plate-glass windows mirroring an urban scene.

Although Estes's paintings look like they were created using a photograph, in fact he used a series of photographic images and selected elements from each. Unlike in actual photographs, however, the images in his paintings are in uniform sharp focus, creating a peculiar Post-modern fusion of mechanical reproduction and reality.[34]

In 1974, architects Richard Rogers and Renzo Piano made literal the idea of escalator as art—and the escalator as conduit to art—in their design for the Pompidou Center in Paris. Situated in the place Beaubourg, the Center became the new home of the Musée Nationale d'Art Moderne and included an audio-visual center and library. Built with a steel-tubed frame and entirely glazed exterior, the Center was designed as a huge exhibition space.

Rogers and Piano's Pompidou Center wears its love of technology on its sleeve. The building frankly exposes its multicolored tubes and ducts, which create a sense of visual play, together with the tubular escalator that zigzags along the building's exterior [147]. Journeying to the center of the museum, visitors also see a sweeping panoramic view of Paris through the escalators' curving glass-covered space.

During the 1980s, 1990s, and into the current century, photographers captured the continuing exuberance of escalator design. Escalators often appear sculptural in their own right, conveying an image of fluidity and grace. In 1985, *Progressive Architecture* predicted that as owners of commercial and institutional buildings became "more image-conscious, the curved escalator will no doubt become a familiar feature," and by the 1990s, the fluid lines and panoramic views presented by spiral escalators were found at a variety of sites including San Francisco's Union Square Center, the Seibu department store in Tsukuba, Japan, and Orchard Point in Singapore [148].[35]

Escalators have continued to evoke artfulness and wit in their design. Created by Mitsubishi in 1997, a fanciful, clear, dome-shaped capsule transports visitors to Tokyo's Edo Museum up the escalator to the museum's main entrance, lending a sense of space-age excitement, expectation, and even mystery to this escalator ride [145]. And joining playfulness and Chinese cultural imagery, Mitsubishi created a large, yellow, dragon-shaped escalator to take visitors to the top of the dam at the Long Quing Xin Gorge, situated 50 miles (80 kilometers) north-west of Beijing [146].

In the shattering aftermath of September 11, 2001, however, photographers recorded a built environment that was cataclysmically changed. Magnum photographers, who had coincidentally gathered in New York on September 10 for a meeting, recorded the horrifying results of that profoundly traumatic day. Photographer Steve McCurry later wrote "I couldn't believe my eyes," yet his images, perhaps better than most, help us to begin to fathom the massive scale and scope of the destruction.[36]

McCurry was in his office in Greenwich Village when the devastation occurred; later he wrote that having the buildings crumble "was like ripping your heart out." He went down to the site the next morning, and one of his most arresting photographic images was that of the lobby of the World Financial Center—the rubble- and dust-covered stairs, the cylindrical concrete pillars, and the escalator—the entire shadowy interior broken only by patches of sunlight [149]. It was "utterly silent" as he photographed the scene, now bereft of people and cloaked only in scraps of paper and beige and gray dust.

In Van Esselstyn's 1940s painting of the escalator, the sunlight beaming down illuminated a world charged with energy and life; Richard Estes's paintings provided images of the escalator as a highly polished emblem of a fast-moving

145 ABOVE
Escalator to the entrance of Edo Museum, Tokyo, 1997. From *Elevator World*, 1997.

146 OPPOSITE
Dragon Escalator, Long Quing Xin Gorge, China, 1997. From *Elevator World*, 1997.

147 **Pompidou Center, Paris, designed by Richard Rogers and Renzo Piano,** *c.* **1977.**

148 Spiral escalators at Creo Shopping Center, Tsukuba, Japan, 1985.

technological society; but in Steve McCurry's photograph of the World Financial Center, the stopped escalator, frozen in time, becomes a grim reminder of wounded and deeply shaken technological dreams.

In today's world, however, technology has not been stilled. There are new transportation designs on the drawing boards as escalator manufacturers prepare to take the next step. Sculptural, colorful, illuminated, and incorporating the latest technologies, these new escalators continue to reshape our visions of transportation—and of art.

149
Steve McCurry, *Two World Financial Center at 6:30 p.m., After the Collapse of World Trade Center's Twin Towers, September 11, 2001, New York.*

1. For a contemporary account of Seeberger's escalator at the Paris Exposition, see "The 'Escalator' or Continuous Elevator" in the British journal *Engineering*, vol. 70, November 30, 1900, pp. 692, 699–700. Jesse Reno also had an escalator of his own design at the Exposition, in addition there were twenty-eight French-built escalators in buildings, but they were designed as moving bands. Otis's escalator was the only one designed as a staircase.

2. For more on speed and nineteenth-century technologies see Julie Wosk, *Breaking Frame: Technology and the Visual Arts in the Nineteenth Century*, New Brunswick, New Jersey (Rutgers University Press) 1992, particularly Chapter Two, "The Traumas of Transport."

3. For a discussion of neoclassical motifs and nineteenth-century steam-engine design, see Wosk, Chapters Three and Five.

4. Even before Reno built the first escalator, in 1859 Nathan Ames of Massachusetts patented a proto-escalator in the form of an endless belt of steps with comb-like plates at the end. For early escalator history, see David A. Cooper, "The History of the Escalator," *Lift Report*, January–February 2000, and William Worthington, Jr., "Early Risers," *Invention and Technology*, Winter 1989, pp. 40–44.

5. "The Reno Inclined Elevator," *Scientific American*, January 16, 1897, p. 41.

6. Reno's early Coney Island escalator and its later use at the Brooklyn Bridge cited in Cooper, p. 64.

7. "The Reno Continuous Passenger Elevator," *Engineering News*, August 25, 1892, pp. 188–89.

8. "The Reno Inclined Elevator," *Scientific American*, January 16, 1897, p. 41.

9. "Traveling Stairways for the Elevated Railways, New York," *Scientific American*, November 17, 1900, p. 313; Cooper, p. 64. A Seeberger escalator became the first one used in a New York subway station, installed in 1906 at the Bowery Station at Delancy Street (Cooper, p. 66).

10. Charles D. Seeberger, "The Escalator," *Cassier's Engineering Monthly*, March 1904, p. 458.

11. "Great Northern, Piccadilly, and Brompton Railway," *The Engineer*, December 14, 1906, p. 598; Ray Orton, London Transport Museum, *Moving People From Street to Platform: 100 Years Underground*, Mobile, Alabama (Elevator World) 2001, pp. 24–26.

12. "London's New Amusement: Up and Down the Escalator," *The Illustrated London News*, October 14, 1911, pp. 592–93; Otis Elevator Company, "The Escalator, Earl's Court Station, London," *The Indicator*, June 1912, vol. 5, no. 6, p. 44.

13. "London's New Amusement," pp. 592–93.

14. "London's New Amusement," pp. 592–93.

15. The photograph and description appear in Otis Elevator Company, *Escalators*, 1912, pp. 9–10 and the image was reprinted in Otis' *Escalators*, 1928, p. 22. See also Cooper, p. 66.

16. Otis Elevator Company, *Escalators*, 1928, p. 23.

17. Otis Elevator Company, *Moving Your Customers and What They Buy. Brief Suggestions for Increasing Business by Increasing Service*, New York, 1915, p. 11.

18. S.P. Ring, "The Escalator for Department Stores," *Architects' and Builders' Magazine*, December 1912, pp. 509–14.

19. "The Reno Inclined Elevator in a Department Store," *The Electrical Engineer*, vol. 26, July 7, 1898, pp. 1–3.

20. Robert Hendrickson, *The Grand Emporiums: Illustrated History of America's Great Department Stores*, New York (Stein and Day) 1979, p. 106.

21. "The Reno Inclined Elevator in a Department Store," pp. 1–2.

22. Cooper, p. 64.

23. Edward Hungerford, *The Romance of a Great Store*, New York (R.M. McBride) 1922, p. 74.

24. Edwin J. Houston, *Electricity in Every-Day Life*, New York (P.F. Collier) 1905, II, photograph opposite p. 442.

25. Otis Elevator Company, *Two-Story 5 & 10 Cent Stores*.

26. Otis Elevator Company brochure, 1922.

27. Umberto Boccioni, Carlo D. Carrà et al., "Technical Manifesto," in *Futurist Manifestos*, April 11, 1910, ed. Embro Apollonio, trans. Robert Brain, New York (Viking Press) pp. 19–24.

28. For studies of streamlining see Jeffrey L. Meikle, *Twentieth-Century Limited: Industrial Design in America, 1925–39*, Second Edition, Philadelphia (Temple University Press) 2001; Donald J. Bush, *The Streamlined Decade*, New York (George Braziller) 1975; and Richard Guy Wilson, "Transportation Machine Design," in *The Machine Age in America, 1918–1941*, New York (Brooklyn Museum of Art/Harry Abrams) 1986, p. 249.

29. Sheldon Cheney and Martha Candler Cheney, *Art and the Machine: An Account of Industrial Design in 20th Century America*, New York (McGraw Hill) 1936, p. 97.

30. Van Esselstyn's written response in 1950 to a New York Metropolitan Museum of Art query (manuscript in the prints and manuscripts collection of the Museum of the City of New York).

31. Jan Seidler Ramirez et al., *Painting the Town: Cityscapes of New York From the Museum of the City of New York*, New Haven, Connecticut (Yale University Press) 2000.

32. For more on Collins and the FSA–OWI women photographers, see Julie Wosk, *Women and the Machine: Representations From the Spinning Wheel to the Electronic Age*, Baltimore (Johns Hopkins University Press) 2001, and Andrea Fisher, *Let Us Now Praise Famous Women: American Women Photographers for the U.S. Government, 1935–44*, London (Pandora) 1987.

33. Louis K. Meisel, *Richard Estes: The Complete Paintings, with an essay by John Perreault*, New York (Abrams) 1986, p. 25.

34. Contemporary critics have argued that Estes's use of photography in his paintings becomes a Post-modern tribute to photography itself—a technological medium, a mechanical means of reproduction which shapes perception.

35. Thomas Fisher, "Spiral Escalators," *Progressive Architecture*, July 1985, p. 137. For more recent spiral designs, see cover story, *Escalator World*, August 2002.

36. *New York September 11 by Magnum Photographers*, New York (PowerHouse Books) 2001. All quotations are from this and wall texts at the New York Historical Society exhibit, "New York, September 11," held from November 2001–February 2002. For an exhibit review, see Julie Wosk, "Photographing Devastation,"

Elevator Stories:
Vertical Imagination and the
Spaces of Possibility

Susan Garfinkel

150
Elevator shaft of the Paul-Löbe Haus, Parliamentary
Committee Chambers, Berlin, designed by Stephan
Braunfels Architects, 2001.

**"This small room, so commonplace and so compressed . . . this elevator
contains them all: space, time, cause, motion, magnitude, class."**
Robert Coover, *The Elevator*[1]

Elevators are spaces at once both mundane and extraordinary. In an early scene
of the film *Being John Malkovich* (1999), hero Craig (John Cusack) has been
instructed to report to the seven-and-a-halfth floor of a building.[2] Puzzled, he
boards the elevator and surveys the familiar whole-number choices on the panel
of buttons before him. "Seven-and-a-half? I'll take you through it," responds a
veteran passenger to his obvious confusion. Then, as the over-door indicator light
passes seven, she abruptly pushes the emergency button, triggering the shrill of
an alarm bell as the elevator jolts to a halt. With a waiting crowbar she pries open
the well-dented steel doors. "Thanks," says Craig, deadpan, as he steps out into
a stooped-over world of four-foot-high ceilings. So begins his very odd adventure
[151–54]. The elevator in *Malkovich* functions as a visible and visceral gateway
between the supposed ordinariness of everyday life and a strange interstitial
world of trapdoors, bodily portals, fleeting fame, and immortality. When Craig
wrests permanent control of actor John Malkovich's body—from Malkovich himself, but also from the group of septuagenarians who plan to live on through

151-154
Four scenes from *Being John Malkovich*, 1999.
Director Spike Jonze, writer Charlie Kaufman,
Gramercy Pictures.

Clockwise, from top left: Prying open the elevator
doors with a crowbar; View of the elevator floor
indicator showing the 7th and 8th floors lit up;
View of the Ripe Vessel; and Craig Schwartz
(John Cusack) stepping out of the elevator on the
7½th floor.

him—it's as if the early wresting of control from the elevator prefigured these larger events. Throughout the action on the seven-and-a-halfth floor, the background chiming of the elevator's bell reminds us of the functional strangeness of this fictive world. The recurring journey within the narrative—from elevator, to tunnel in the wall, to Malkovich's mind, to a stretch of grass beside the Jersey Turnpike—affirms that technology can serve as a non-standard but still effective gateway to the soul. Lest we fail to notice this, the film provides an iconographic image of "the ripe vessel" as artery-cum-tunnel on which to hang the set of transformations [153].

Elevators, and the networks of shafts and vents that house them, are to our buildings like veins and arteries to the body—conduits that permeate and structure the spaces of our lives, while still remaining separate from the fixity of happenings around them. Nearby yet hidden from view, always in motion, temporary shelter to an ever-changing cast of characters, guided as if by some invisible force, elevators have become an accustomed part of our everyday existence. If they are sometimes mechanically unsound, arrive and depart too quickly, bear surprising visitors, or force strangers into too-close proximity, this only enhances the edgy, dizzying quality they so easily evoke in fictional presentations. The tightness of the car is by turns inviting or confining, a comfortable enclosure or a space of anxiety and discomfort, while its mundane interior affords the camera a variety of challenging visual perspectives. If its doors open up to us the secrets of interior space, they also make us into unsuspecting voyeurs when we look in or stare out. The shaftways, vents, and mechanisms that surround the cars are dark and deserted as tombs, or sparkling technological playgrounds for the eye.

If we tend to use elevators in our daily lives without concern, when we are invited through art or artifice to stop and take notice we just as often find these accustomed spaces marked as sites of strange encounters, unusual coincidences, near escapes, dangerous accidents, or sudden malice. With their contingent yet central location and transient yet inclusive cast of characters, elevators function as spaces of possibility, fully ready to transport us beyond the commonplace. It is no doubt for this reason that the space of the elevator has consistently been used as a transition point, visual cue, plot device, or primary setting in literature and on the screen.

An aura of expectation surrounds elevators. Public yet private, enclosing yet permeable, separate from but integral to the architectural spaces that surround them, they invite us to expect the unexpected in certain predictable ways. Here we will focus on the "betweenness" of elevator space—its conditional, transitional, and interstitial qualities—as depicted in film and fiction.[3] While the twentieth century brought us urbanization, mechanization, and the alienation that accompanied them, we increasingly face the breakdown of its familiar pairings of man and machine. Now our thoughts turn instead toward questions of interpenetration, and of what's real and how we know it. Through a series of encounters (commonplaces and spectacles, destinations and thresholds, journeys and juxtapositions) we explore here the contours of experience in ever-shifting elevator space. Transporting us in imagination as they do in the world, elevators offer a unique yet still familiar means of exploring our potential connections to the present, to the future, to possibility, and to each other.

Encounters: The Commonplace

Just as the design of elevators and their position within an architectural framework inform the ways that we use them—making us wait or hurry, granting or limiting our access to certain parts of a building—they also inform the uses that artists, authors, and filmmakers have found for elevators in fiction and in film.

In *Grand Hotel* (1932), elevators are featured as a conspicuous mark of luxury, yet also provide a convenient device for recurring transitions between scenes.[4] In *Elevator to the Gallows* (1957), a stalled elevator car serves style as well as plot when, illuminated only by the flame of the protagonist's cigarette lighter, it provides the camera a chance to explore contrasting light and shadows to classic film-noir effect [156].[5] In the comedy *Switching Channels* (1987), the actor Christopher Reeves's hilarious acrophobic breakdown in a glass-sided elevator car stands on its own, but also proves the turning point in his pretentious character's bid to retain the affection of the movie's heroine.[6] In *Prizzi's Honor* (1985), a woman steps from an elevator to a gun pointed right at her head. "I must have the wrong floor," she says in her last moments.[7] These scenes all work because we expect the uneventful in certain predictable ways. If the elevator brings death in one scene of a movie, it still brings a swift and unremarkable ride in another, with the result that we are always open to surprise.

A scene from *Serendipity* (2001) highlights the way in which even the most everyday "dangers" of an elevator ride can have dramatic consequences.[8] Jonathan (John Cusack) and Sara (Kate Beckinsale) meet while shopping in New York City and spend a romantic evening together. Unsure of what comes next, they decide to test fate by stepping into facing elevators in the busy Waldorf–Astoria Hotel. If they each pick the same floor they will meet again above; if not, they go their separate ways. While Sara's choice is deliberate and serene, Jonathan's is agonized and random, yet each presses the same button: 23. Sara has an uninterrupted ride and steps out from her elevator with certainty, but Jonathan's progress is quickly disrupted. His elevator stops to let on a father and his hyperactive son—dressed for a party in a devil's costume—who pushes every button on the panel. As Jonathan gesticulates, the camera cuts to views of him and a changing cast of fellow passengers running out at each floor, looking right and left with expectation, then crowding back into the elevator before the door has closed. Disappointed, Sara finally summons an elevator down; it comes instantly and closes on her departing form just seconds before Jonathan arrives. Of course, such near misses easily build suspense, and are a common motif that takes advantage of the elevator's inherent qualities.

The illusion created by the elevator is one of bringing the different strata of a building's spaces together. Riders have agency, but lack ultimate control over their choice of traveling companions or their moment of arrival or departure. Classes, races, and ages mix together. Doors slide open and close according to their own preordained priorities, seemingly choosing companions for us, or affording us a pleasant moment of privacy. In daily life we manage these contingencies by building in buffers of time and space—leaving early to allow for unforeseen delays, putting on public faces that encourage interaction, or not, as we prefer. Once aboard we space ourselves out as much as possible with each change of personnel, but we also allow ourselves to be squeezed against strangers without flinching [155]. As a narrator of the short computer animation *Elevator World* (2000) states, "A rectangular retreat . . . opens its gates beckoning all to come. The downtrodden and the upwardly mobile ride together in total equality, watching numbers. Yes, welcome to Elevator World."[9] In this four-minute presentation, a blithely ironic tone but insightful understanding of the elevator's issues humorously condense our everyday experience of the elevator ride.

Spectacle: Technology and Danger

Elevators have long been associated with danger and spectacle. Perhaps it was the theatricality of Elisha Graves Otis's original presentation at the 1853–54 Crystal Palace Exposition that set the stage for future depictions. In his novel

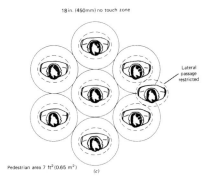

155 ABOVE
Pedestrians queuing in elevators. From George R. Strakosch, ed., *The Vertical Transportation Handbook*, 3rd edn New York (John Wiley & Sons, Inc.) 1998.

156 OPPOSITE
Julien Tavernier (Maurice Ronet) trying to escape from an elevator, from *Elevator to the Gallows*, 1958. Director Louis Malle, writer Louis Malle, based on the novel by Noël Calef. Nouvelles Editions de Films (France).

157-180 **Panorama from the Eiffel Tower at the Paris Exposition Universelle, 1900.**

181-204 **Panorama of the moving sidewalk at the Paris Exposition Universelle, 1900.**

The Intuitionist (1999), Colson Whitehead captures the drama of that foundational event:

"The platform rises thirty feet in the air, grasping for the glass dome above . . . . "Please watch carefully," Mr. Otis says. He holds a saw in the air, a gold crescent in the lamplight, and begins to sever the rope holding him . . . . The rope dances in the air as the final strands give. The platform falls eternally for a foot or two before the old wagon spring underneath the platform releases and catches in the ratchets of the guard rails. The people in the Exhibition still have a roar in them . . . . Mr. Elisha Otis removes his top hat with a practiced flourish and says, "All safe, gentlemen, all safe."[10]

Certainly Whitehead sees a resonance between that history and his fictional present, circa 1965, where the thuglike head of the Department of Elevator Inspectors re-enacts this moment of Otis's triumph at the inspectors' yearly pageant. This time, however, the self-important Chancre finds himself the victim of sabotage and a resultant broken leg. This failure foreshadows a broader shakeup of the entire elevator industry.

Spectacle is central to one of Thomas Edison's Paris Exposition films of 1900, in which footage tracks the view from an elevator car as it travels up inside one leg of the Eiffel Tower [157–180].[11] While we see nothing more extraordinary than an ever-widening vista of buildings and boulevards, the view interrupted only by the tower's structural elements, for 1900 the fact of this bird's-eye view was extraordinary all in itself. So too was the dual celebration of moving transport and moving pictures that the short film embodies. Many of Edison's films are explorations of motion from different viewpoints and angles: a parade of cars in one, the flow of Niagara Falls in another. Two films of the moving sidewalk at the Paris Exposition seem an early exploration of relativity: in one the camera travels along with the moving sidewalk; in the second it remains stationary while motion is provided by the ever-approaching stream of passengers [181–204].[12]

Elevators show up early and often in commercial films of the twentieth century, as markers of urbanity, grandeur, or the future. But elevator spectacle comes into its own in the second half of the century, concomitant with the presence of automatic elevators in increasingly higher rise buildings. Such thrillers as *The Towering Inferno* (1974), *De Lift* (1983), *Die Hard* (1988), and *Speed* (1994) take advantage of the dependence of tall buildings on their elevators, and of their vulnerability to natural disaster or purposeful attack [205].[13] The opening sequence of *Speed* is a celebration of gleaming steel and well-oiled hydraulic machinery, as cables and cars move silently through visually pristine spaces [150]. When hero John McClane (Bruce Willis) sets an elevator shaft on fire in *Die Hard*, the result is a visually stunning cyclone of bright flames that sweeps through the vertical space and out the roof into the sky above.

Other films use the techno-laden space of the elevator shaft to a variety of emotional advantages, as in *Elevator to the Gallows*, where the film's protagonist is delayed at a crucial moment when the power has been shut off for the night. After an excruciating scene where he lowers himself through the elevator's trap door and is nearly crushed when the power is suddenly restored, the man, who has just committed a murder, is forced to spend the night in close proximity to the scene of his crime. By contrast, in *Toy Story 2* (1999) the shaft's visibility is treated in a lighthearted fashion when a group of animated toys climb up an elevator shaft instead of taking the next available car.[14] By enacting a familiar scenario of gratuitous danger and heroism, the *Toy Story* characters indulge our fascination with hidden elevator technology to charmingly comedic effect. As, over time, the elevator's mechanisms have become increasingly hidden from

205
Spanish-language movie poster for *De Lift* (The Lift), 1983. Director and writer Dick Maas, First Floor Features (The Netherlands).

Fran Kubelik (Shirley MacLaine) pinning a flower on Calvin Clifford "C.C." "Bud" Baxter (Jack Lemmon) outside the elevator, from *The Apartment*, 1960. Director Billy Wilder, writers Billy Wilder and I.A.L. Diamond, Mirisch Company/Metro-Goldwyn-Mayer Inc.

Fran and Bud with others in the elevator, from *The Apartment*, 1960.

passengers, visual access only works to enhance our voyeuristic pleasure in the moment.[15]

Destinations: Upward Mobility and the Vertigo of Success

Sometimes what's most interesting about an elevator is where it's going, and who it's taking there. Literature and film, like real life earlier in the twentieth century, are amply populated with elevator operators, attendants, repairmen, and inspectors [214]. These are the men and women who navigate elevators for us, but who also dwell in them in characteristic ways. One critic notes the recurring theme of elevator-boy-turned-aspiring-self-made-man in German stories about American-style cities—even Kafka wrote about an elevator boy.[16] Although young boys operated elevators through the end of the nineteenth century, American child-labor laws ended the practice. In American treatments today, the elevator operator is adult, and just as likely a woman or person of color as a white male down on his luck. The correlation of the role of the servant with race and gender in American society makes equivocating depictions more realistic, if less hopeful [211]. Yet the issue of status—achieved or merely desired—is frequently explored through the operator's job, even if upward mobility is only an intermittent dream.

A number of prominent African-American writers had early jobs as elevator operators, including Langston Hughes who published a well-known poem on the subject.[17] Paul Laurence Dunbar, born in 1872, was known as the elevator boy poet because, when racism prevented him from finding more appropriate work, he sold his published poems from his elevator car.[18] The literary association of black people with elevators has a certain lasting resonance, as in Whitehead's *The Intuitionist,* where heroine Lila Mae Watson's father had a degree in engineering and a love of elevators, but could never find employment beyond a degrading operator's job in a department store. Lila Mae, in turn, is the first woman and only the second black person to become a licensed elevator inspector in the country's tallest city, but her life, despite her achievement, is empty and forlorn. The novel uses her story to engage in a complex analysis of racial mobility through the promises of elevator technology.

In Hollywood, the bit part of elevator operator was one of the few movie roles open to black male actors before the 1960s. In an interesting twist, the movie version of Richard Wright's *Native Son* (1951)—in which the author himself plays tragic hero Bigger Thomas—substitutes Bigger's graphic murder of his girlfriend by bludgeoning with an equally violent if less visibly gory shove down an elevator shaft.[19] Though the switch between novel and movie reflects the decade's filmic sensibilities, the choice of the elevator shaft as symbolic of the black man's oppression is surely purposeful.

In film the "corporate ladder" is visually symbolized by the corporate elevator. *The Apartment* (1960) features the budding romance between Fran Kubelik (Shirley MacLaine), an engaging elevator operator in a highly regulated insurance office building, and Bud Baxter (Jack Lemmon), the too-sincere junior executive roped into lending his bachelor apartment to various supervisors for their extra-marital trysts [207]. In exchange for these favors he's been promised speedy job advancement.[20] When called upstairs for his first promotion, Baxter ducks into Fran's elevator with a newfound boldness, excitedly explaining his errand. "You know," Fran compliments him as she ferries him from 9 up to 27, "you're the only one around here who ever takes his hat off in the elevator." He responds with a compliment in turn: "That's the first thing I ever noticed about you, when you were still on the local elevator—you always wore a flower" [206]. Eventually the big boss gets involved in the apartment-borrowing scheme, but this married man also turns out to be dating Fran in secret, stringing her along. When Baxter must

choose between an upper-floor office and his feelings for Fran, his choice becomes clear. Bud and Fran quit their jobs, and their corporate elevator games are left happily behind.

Other mid-century depictions show the psychological struggles of the elevator operator. In John Cheever's story, "Christmas is a Sad Season for the Poor" (1978), familyless elevator man Charlie bridles at working on Christmas day among the wealthy tenants of an upscale New York apartment building:

"He, Charlie, was a prisoner, confined eight hours a day to a six-by-eight elevator cage, which was confined, in turn, to a sixteen-story shaft. In one building or another he had made his living as an elevator operator for ten years. He estimated the average trip at about an eighth of a mile, and when he thought of the thousands of miles he had traveled, when he thought [that] he might have driven the car through the mists above the Caribbean and set it down on some coral beach in Bermuda, he held the narrowness of his travels against his passengers, as if it was not the nature of the elevator but the pressure of their lives that confined him, as if they had clipped his wings."[21]

Charlie shares his woes, and without fail his passengers take pity. By mid-afternoon he has fourteen trays of food in his locker room, "and the bell just kept ringing. Just as he started to eat one, he would have to go up and get another." Though he could barely begin to eat the food, Charlie drinks everything that is offered him, and by mid-afternoon is enjoying the effects of the alcohol:

"His face was blazing. He loved the world, and the world loved him . . . . He thought that his job as an elevator operator—cruising up and down through hundreds of feet of perilous space—demanded the nerve and the intellect of a birdman . . . . [H]e got into the elevator and shot it at full speed up to the penthouse and down again, up and down, to test his wonderful mastery of space."[22]

Yet very soon it all comes to an end, when a passenger appears and Charlie fails to constrain himself appropriately: "With his hands off the controls in a paroxysm of joy [he] shouted 'Strap on your safety belt, Mrs. Gadshill! We're going to make a loop-the-loop!'"[23] Though previously sympathetic to Charlie's plight, Mrs. Gadshill now runs screaming to his boss. Charlie is fired on the spot. He discovers there is no way to love this job and maintain it, both at once.

Two late-century films about sudden corporate success reinforce the easy link between job status and elevator use, relying on the physical ride upward as a metaphor for dramatic rise in status. In *The Secret of My Success* (1987), Michael J. Fox plays Brantley Foster, a recent college graduate who gets a mailroom job in the big-city business of his uncle [208].[24] Feeling his talents have been grossly overlooked, he co-opts an empty upper-floor office to pretend he's the company's newest executive, working into the night to develop his own financial strategy. By day he careens frantically between his two jobs, changing outfits in the elevator and getting caught on more than one occasion. In the process of solving the company's fiscal woes he also wins as his girlfriend an aloof but beautiful female executive, and the elevator functions as a setting for his courtship through handy use of the emergency brake.

The *Hudsucker Proxy* (1994) is a darkly brilliant reworking of the classic success story [209].[25] Tim Robbins plays Norville Barnes, a foolish business-school grad who comes to New York for a job, circa 1958. Norville lands in the mailroom of massive Hudsucker Industries just as upstairs company president Waring Hudsucker (Charles Durning) throws himself out the boardroom window. The film, governed by a retro aesthetic and a penchant for absurdity, turns success on its head when goofy Norville, soon ferried to the top floor by obnoxious Buzz the elevator boy, is named president of Hudsucker to scare off would-be

185

208 ABOVE
Brantley Foster aka Carlton Whitfield (Michael J. Fox) getting changed in the elevator, from *The Secret of My Success*, 1987. Director Herbert Ross, writers A.J. Carothers and Jim Cash, Universal Pictures.

209 OPPOSITE
Norville Barnes (Tim Robbins) and Buzz the elevator operator (Jim True-Frost) with others in the elevator, from *The Hudsucker Proxy*, 1994. Directors and writers Joel and Ethan Coen, Silver Pictures/Warner Brothers.

investors. Hoping to throw the company into failure so that they can buy up all its stock, the board of directors allows Norville to manufacture his odd invention—"You know, for kids"—but when this Hula-Hoop stand-in turns successful they are thwarted. Next Buzz is bribed to ruin Norville with a public scandal, so that the elevator boy ushers in Norville's fall as well as his rise. In a gorgeous scene of prolonged vertigo, Norville jumps from the boardroom window himself, but lands suspended in mid air when the building's big clock sticks and time stands still. His earthward plunge thus interrupted, Norville is visited by Mr. Hudsucker-turned-angel who floats down from Heaven to give him the pep talk that saves him. The exaggerated perspective and architectural beauty that accompany Norville's fall dramatically reinforce the message of status, height, and vertigo that the film so elegantly satirizes.

Thresholds: Within and Between

A threshold, in concrete terms that narrow strip beneath the frame of a doorway, can also refer to any sort of space that contains the moment of crossing from place to place, or from one state of being to another. We can think of the elevator as a sort of movable threshold that—because of the necessities of gravity— stretches out that crossing point in a suspended moment of time as well as space. Sometimes, however, the transitional quality of the elevator is not as neutral as we might expect. Television sitcoms, including *All in the Family* and *Night Court,* have featured episodes where babies are born in stuck elevators and otherwise curmudgeonly cast members turn out to have hearts of gold.[26] In film, when Hal Larson (Jack Black) in *Shallow Hal* (2001) is hypnotized in a broken-down elevator, he emerges with a newfound view of the world.[27] In Ingmar Bergman's *Secrets of Women* (1952), a couple's attempt to heal their marriage lasts no longer than the time they are stuck in an elevator together.[28] On a grimmer note, in *Silence of the Lambs* (1991) murderer Hannibal Lecter (Anthony Hopkins) kills one of his prison guards, swaps outfits, and throws the body into the elevator shaft.[29] Now disguised as the wounded guard, Lecter is transported to an ambulance below. Since the dead body landed on the roof of the elevator car, blood begins to drip down through its ceiling, distracting police as Lecter is whisked away, escaping to his first taste of freedom in years. Through this intricate ruse, the elevator works to carry him from captivity to freedom as surely as if he were an ordinary passenger.

Sometimes elevators get stuck, but sometimes extend their betweenness when they just keep going and going. The paternoster elevator reinforces this point with its series of continuously moving open cars joined in a circuit— passengers must jump on and off at just the right instant. In Robert Coover's story *The Elevator*, fourteen short sections correspond to the daily musings of a man on his way to the office on the fourteenth floor.[30] With each reiteration of the disarmingly varied yet still recognizable ride—in one he is teased by fellow passengers, in another he goes down instead of up, in a third he flirts with an imaginary elevator girl, and in a fourth has sex with her as the car enters free fall—it is increasingly less clear if these iterations are daydreams, fantasies, or alternate realities that somehow coexist.

In the short Canadian play *Elevator* by Cherie Stewart (1975), two older women meet in the elevator of their apartment building and spend an afternoon riding together.[31] Katie, who hasn't been outside in five years, runs a business from the elevator itself: coffee and muffins in the morning, cocktails in the evening [210]. "Real cream for the coffee," she explains. "Have a coffee and muffin on your way to work. Great idea. I've done well." Though she and Martha have never met, they are both veterans of the overlong elevator ride. "Aren't you getting off?" asks Martha. "After you," Katie retorts. But down at the lobby Martha

210
Elevator in the Old State Capitol, Olympia, Washington, designed by Willis Ritchie, 1892.

discovers it's raining and steps right back in. They discuss Katie's patrons: "Sometimes they ride up and down with me for fifteen minutes," she explains. "Till they finish." "That settles it," declares Martha, "I'm not going out today."

Having abruptly cancelled her plans, Martha brings in chairs while Katie fetches costumes and the ingredients for punch. As the women practice their lines for the upcoming cocktail hour, the enclosing space of the elevator car becomes womblike in its rhythmic protectiveness. Sheltering them from their fears of the larger outside world, as they sample multiple cups of punch, it in turn becomes a safe space for their deviance. No longer rivals, the women seal their new bond of friendship when they yell out curse words in celebratory unison. Since the play ends before any neighbors-turned-patrons appear, any negative effects of the afternoon's drunken ride are left unexplored.

In the short story *The Enormous Radio* (1953) by John Cheever, an elevator's penetration into the darkest reaches of shared space leaves neighbors on less pleasant terms. When young wife Irene's pricey new radio malfunctions, it res-onates with her apartment building's elevator shaft:

"The rattling of the elevator cables and the opening and closing of the elevator doors were reproduced by her loudspeaker, and, realizing that the radio was sensitive to electrical currents of all sorts, she began to discern through the Mozart the ringing of telephone bells, the dialing of phones, and the lamentation of a vacuum cleaner. By listening more carefully, she was able to distinguish doorbells, elevator bells, electric razors, and Waring mixers, whose sounds had been picked up from the apartments that surrounded hers . . . ."[32]

Though a repairman visits, Irene next discovers that she can hear the voices of her neighbors just as clearly. She and husband Jim stay up late listening in on conversations by turns silly, mean, pathetic, tedious, dishonest, and brutal. As Irene becomes obsessed with the sordid lives of those around her, the elevator becomes the site not just of her visible encounters, but also her secret encoun-ters with her neighbors. "There were a number of women in the elevator when it stopped at her floor. She stared at their handsome and impassive faces, their furs, and the cloth flowers in their hats. Which one of them had been to Sea Island, she wondered. Which one had overdrawn her bank account?"[33] There in the elevator, the source of her secret aural knowledge, she can no longer trust these visible public selves. Irene's sense of privacy is shattered.

Journeys: To Heaven, to Hell, to Japan

As the exploration of extended thresholds suggests, sometimes it's not the end-point but the process that matters. In *Deconstructing Harry* (1997), Woody Allen's neurotic and fragmented novelist character descends in an elevator through the various levels of Hell.[34] As Harry passes each floor he hears just what kind of increasingly evil but slightly humorous person resides there. Arriving at the bottom—level nine—he enters an Hieronymus Bosch-style world of swirling smoke and half-dressed natives, lit in bright red lights and looking much like a stage set. There he finds his long-suffering father and his best friend who turns out to be the Devil himself. Then the scene changes and Harry is back in the midst of his car trip, on the way to accept an honorary degree from his alma mater, with his kidnapped son, an overdressed hooker, and a soon-to-be-dead friend in tow. One sort of journey flows into another, suggesting that in meaningful terms they are not as different as we might think.

Allen, of course, was neither the first nor last to settle on the elevator as vehi-cle of choice for reaching Hell at one extreme, or Heaven at the other. In *Heaven Can Wait* (1943) the hero recounts the story of his wicked life, expecting entry into Hades, yet when he's finished the devil escorts him to an elevator with a

one-word instruction: "Up."[35] In *The Horn Blows at Midnight* (1945), Jack Benny plays the third trumpeter in the heavenly orchestra, chosen to descend to Earth and sound the note that will signal the end of the world.[36] He descends through a hotel elevator, but is recognized in the lobby by fallen angels who prevent him from accomplishing his task. More recently, in the short film *The Lift* (2000),[37] Jack and Liz die on their wedding day to discover that the afterlife is a corporate world where the levels of Heaven and Hell are connected by an elevator—and they have both landed on different floors. The focus is on the process rather than the endpoint in Rolf Becker's German novel *Nocturno 1951*. In it his liftboy hero dreams that he must sort his passengers and escort them to Heaven or Hell accordingly. But the scene becomes a nightmare:

"One of the 'bad ones' interfered with the ascent to heaven and hence prevented it! . . . The 'good ones' were not upset at the unrightful presence of the 'bad one.' They all stood in the narrow lift cage and ignored each other. . . . The last thing that happened . . . he grabbed for the lever and pushed it down, and the lift sunk and went off course, but did not crash, but floated downwards, 'to hell,' with all those chosen and him . . . even farther downwards into a bottomless abyss."[38]

Here Hell becomes a nameless void that confounds the social order, so that the usual protections of limited access no longer apply [212].

Perhaps older legends about journeys to the afterlife first inspired the idea of an elevator serving to cross from this world to the next. Colson Whitehead writes, "There's an old inspector's maxim: 'An Elevator is a grave,'" though elsewhere in his novel elevators function as wombs, trains, or "stepping stones to Heaven, which make relentless verticality so alluring."[39] From the ancient Greek legend of the boatman Charon, to John Bunyan's *Pilgrim's Progress* and Dante's *Inferno*, to Michael rowing his boat ashore in song, the process of dying has involved the work of *traveling* from this life to the next. Even in the quintessential near-death experience, movement down a long, lighted tunnel is not unlike the sensation of movement we experience, or imagine, in a long and swift elevator ride. What the elevator adds to our vision of above and below is the strength of its verticality and the customary disjunction between its starting and its end points. Arriving in the afterlife probably *is* like an elevator ride.

In Maude Hutchins's unusual short story *The Elevator* (1962), the destination is Japan, the setting is dreamlike, and the process of travel is a journey of artistic re-creation. The story is told by a female narrator:

"I wore a black dinner dress with pearls around my neck and very high heels that frightened me. . . . My fingers seemed longer than usual and more flexible . . . . I rang again, daintily pushing the bell that said UP and as I did so, the elevator, a blaze of bluish light, plunged downward and a sort of vertigo made me feel that at last I was on the way."[40]

At stops along the swift ascent—"the floors were racing by so fast that the numbers ran into each other"—she is joined successively by a literal cast of unusual characters, including at last the man who has imagined all the others, the author.[41] The flow of the journey—its strangeness, height, evolution of purpose, and eventually the premise of an author negotiating his latest work of fiction—transports the reader as the elevator does. When a character is rejected, the elevator stops: "The old guy can take the fire escape down"; and when the dialogue strays the elevator man interrupts: "We're off course."[42] As the piece ends we find that the elevator ride is a metaphor for the delivery of a conclusion, as the narrative dissolves in an exploration of stereotypes and language games. This elevator goes not to Heaven or Hell, but to elsewhere, though the process is similarly fraught.

212
Oliver Herford, *Down*, c. 1916.

Juxtapositions: Sliding Doors and Uncertain Futures

Elevators allow us to move quickly between places that are literally as well as conceptually far apart, shifting levels or directions at short notice, changing scenes and spaces in a way that was formerly impossible. The short ride from a quiet office down to a busy lobby can be jarring without an appropriate mental shift of gears. The invisibility of an elevator's mechanisms only heightens the disorientation we experience when scenes and contexts shift too quickly. Just as elevators have helped us to negotiate a sort of everyday relativity between spaces, times, and situations, our familiarity with their uses in the making of stories can help us to make sense of increasingly complicated lives. In recent years, the Post-modern world has been defined as one of slippage, fragmentation, disjunction, and juxtaposition. Though its history is much longer, our experience with the changeable elevator over time can help to move our stories into the complicated present.

In Post-modern life, motifs or images can decorate the surfaces of things, but may or may not correspond to the more important underlying meanings. In the screenplay for MURDER and murder (1996), slapstick humor is juxtaposed with the very real trauma caused by breast cancer and its treatment in order to illustrate the loss of control a patient feels at the hands of the medical establishment. As if to highlight the system's madness and the patient's disorientation, characters appear in various outlandish costumes to perform a caricature of a Keystone Kops elevator chase—only here the "cops" are dressed as doctors. As the action proceeds:

"[T]he COP/DOCS manage to push YOUNG MILDRED and JENNY against the elevator doors. They gesticulate wildly, resisting blame for whatever charges are being pressed on them. The elevator doors open and MILDRED, DORIS, JEFFREY, and ALICE, plus a half-dozen women wearing huge breast prostheses over wild costumes, burst out. There are a Brunnhilde, a bearded bride, and various mismatched stereotypes."[43]

This elevator slapstick brings visual form to social commentary, revealing a system that is real but ought to be strange, juxtaposing camp with larger social issues.

In *Sliding Doors* (1998), Gwyneth Paltrow plays Helen, a woman whose life changes dramatically after she drops her earring in an elevator.[44] This delays her arrival at the subway, which causes her to miss the train that would have allowed her to walk in on her boyfriend's infidelity. Except that, in the fictive world of the movie, the scene rewinds and this time Helen just makes it aboard the train [213]. There she talks with James (John Hannah), who saw her on the elevator before, and who soon becomes the focus of her affections. The movie then traces the parallel lives of both Helens: one still with her philandering boyfriend, the other happily with James, until the wiser and happier Helen dies in an accident and the dual identities merge. Yet when the first Helen encounters James in the hospital elevator minutes later, we see that the slippage between her parallel selves has brought her, if unconsciously, to the same psychic turning point that her wiser self had reached. As Helen, now whole, and James turn to face each other with a smile of odd recognition, the closing of the elevator door on their happy future doubles as the screen wipe that ends the film. The automatic doors so frequently encountered serve as a metaphor for change throughout the film, suggesting that while the experience of daily life is often experienced as split-second timing, there may also be deeper patterns that run beneath the surface.

Other recent films have explored versions of a Post-modern slippage between realities, dreams, or wishful projections using varying visual or thematic motifs. In the animated *Monsters, Inc.* (2001), for example, a brilliant chase scene exploits the premise that closet doors are portals from the monster world into

213
Helen Quilley (Gwyneth Paltrow) and James Hammerton (John Hannah) seated in a London Underground car, from *Sliding Doors*, 1998. Director and writer Peter Howitt, Miramax Films.

the human one, as characters jump in and out of parallel locations while the doors sail past along moving storage racks like so many items of neatly bagged dry cleaning.[45] With its sliding doors that so fully embody surprise, the elevator was Post-modern long before there was a label for it.

Elevators have played a surprisingly key role in film and fiction, as intriguing visual component and important spatial setting. They move us through the narrative possibilities of public and private imaginings, through a shared imagery of remembered encounters or the singularity of our personal interpretations. As elevators and their uses have changed with time, so have their depictions in uniquely marked ways. It takes more to surprise us now, but for the sake of entertainment the surprises keep coming. Perhaps it is the extent to which our lives have been permeated by these everyday technologies that invites this heightened level of treatment. Perhaps our familiarity requires increasingly complex representations to hold our interest. More satisfying is the idea that the creative thinkers who help us to interpret our lives through their fiction and film find extraordinary meaning in the everyday precisely because it is there. As spaces of possibility that we encounter every day, elevators simply remind us that our lives are always—and fortunately—subject to change.

214

Elevator operator in the Barr Building, Washington, D.C., 1941.

Elevator Stories

1. Robert Coover, "The Elevator," *Pricksongs and Descants: Fictions*, New York (E.P. Dutton) 1969, p. 44.

2. *Being John Malkovich,* director Spike Jonze, writer Charlie Kaufman, 1999, Gramercy Pictures.

3. The idea of betweenness, or liminality, originates in the field of anthropology. See Arnold van Gennep, *The Rights of Passage*, trans. Monika B. Vizedom and Gabrielle L. Caffe, London (Routledge & Paul) 1960; Victor Turner, *The Ritual Process: Structure and Anti-Structure*, Chicago (Aldine Publishing Co.) 1969.

4. *Grand Hotel*, director Edmund Goulding, writers Vicki Baum and William A. Drake, 1932, Metro-Goldwyn-Mayer.

5. *Elevator to the Gallows* (*Ascenseur pour l'échafaud*), director Louis Malle, screenplay Loius Malle and Roger Nimier, based on a novel by Noël Calef (1956), 1957, Nouvelles Editions de Films.

6. *Switching Channels,* director Ted Kotcheff, writers Ben Hecht, Charles MacArthur, and Jonathan Reynolds, 1988, TriStar Pictures.

7. *Prizzi's Honor*, director John Huston, writers Richard Condon and Janet Roach, 1985, American Broadcasting Company (ABC).

8. *Serendipity*, director Peter Chelsom, writer Marc Klein, 2001, Simon Fields Productions/Tapestry Films/Miramax.

9. Mitchell Rose, *Elevator World*, computer-animated short film, at http://atomfilms.shockwave.com/af/content/atom_331.

10. Colson Whitehead, *The Intuitionist*, New York (Anchor Books) 1999, pp. 81–82.

11. *Panoramic view from the Eiffel Tower, ascending and descending*, Thomas A. Edison, Inc.; producer, James White, 1900, http://hdl.loc.gov/loc.mbrsmi/edmp.1847.

12. *Panaroma from the moving boardwalk*, Thomas A. Edison, Inc.; producer James White, 1900, http://hdl.loc.gov/loc.mbrsmi/edmp.1761; *Panorama of the moving boardwalk*, Thomas A. Edison, Inc.; producer, James White, 1900, http://hdl.loc.gov/loc.mbrsmi/edmp.1771.

13. *The Towering Inferno*, directors Irwin Allen and John Guillermin, writers Richard Martin Stern and Thomas N. Scortia et al., 1974, 20th Century Fox. *De Lift*, director and writer Dick Maas, 1983, First Floor Features (The Netherlands). *Die Hard*, director John McTiernan, writers Roderick Thorp and Jeb Stuart et al., 1988, 20th Century Fox. *Speed*, director Jan de Bont, writer Graham Yost, 1994, 20th Century Fox.

14. *Toy Story 2,* directors John Lasseter et al., writers John Lasseter et al., 1999, Pixar Animation Studies/Walt Disney Pictures.

15. For discussions of architecture in film see: Charles Affron and Mirella Jona Affron, *Sets in Motion: Art Direction and Film Narrative*, New Brunswick, New Jersey (Rutgers University Press) 1995; Mark Lamster (ed.), *Architecture and Film*, New York (Princeton Architectural Press) 2000; Mark Shiel and Rony Fitzmaurice (eds.), *Cinema and the City: Film and Urban Societies in a Global Context*, Oxford (Blackwell) 2001.

16. Eckhard Gruber, "The Yankee Loves the Lift," *Lift Elevator Paternoster: A Cultural History of Vertical Transport*, Berlin, Germany (Ernst & Sohn) 1994, pp. 90–105; Franz Kafka, *Amerika*, trans. Willa and Edwin Muir, New York (Schocken Books) 1996.

17. Langston Hughes, "Elevator Boy," in *Fire!! A Quarterly Devoted to the Younger Negro Artists*, vol. 1, no. 1, November 1926, p. 20. Reprint: Westport, Connecticut (Negro University Press) 1970.

18. Ann Deines, "Paul Laurence Dunbar," *Cultural Resource Management* 5, 1999, pp. 30–31.

19. Richard Wright, *Native Son*, New York (Harper & Brothers) 1940. *Native Son*, director Pierre Chenal, writers Pierre Chenal and Richard Wright, 1950, Argentina Sono Film S.A.C.I.

20. *The Apartment*, director Billy Wilder, writers Billy Wilder and I.A.L. Diamond, 1960, Mirisch Company/Metro-Goldwyn-Mayer Inc.

21. John Cheever, "Christmas is a Sad Season for the Poor," *The Stories of John Cheever*, New York (Knopf) 1978, pp. 128–136.

22. Cheever, *Christmas*, p. 134.

23. Cheever, *Christmas*, p. 134.

24. *The Secret of My Success*, director Herbert Ross, writers A.J. Carothers et al., 1987, Rastar Pictures/Universal Pictures.

25. *The Hudsucker Proxy*, directors and writers Joel Coen and Ethan Coen, 1994, Silver Pictures/Warner Brothers.

26. *All in the Family*, 1971–79, CBS; *Night Court*, 1984–92, NBC.

27. *Shallow Hal*, directors Bobby Farrelly and Peter Farrelly, writers Sean Moynihan, Bobby Farrelly, and Peter Farrelly, 2001, Conundrum Entertainment/20th Century Fox.

28. *Secrets of Women (Kvinnors väntan)*, director and writer Ingmar Bergman, 1952, Svensk Filmindustri (SF) AB.

29. *The Silence of the Lambs*, director Jonathan Demme, writer Ted Tally, based on a novel by Thomas Harris (1988), 1991, Orion Pictures Corporation.

30. Coover, *The Elevator*.

31. Cherie Stewart, *One Spring Morning; Elevator: Two One-Act Plays*, Toronto (Playwrights Co-op) 1975.

32. John Cheever, "The Enormous Radio," *The Stories of John Cheever*, New York (Knopf) 1978, p. 34.

33. Cheever, *The Enormous Radio*, p. 37–38.

34. *Deconstructing Harry*, director and writer Woody Allen, 1997, Sweetland Films.

35. *Heaven Can Wait*, director Ernst Lubitsch, writer Samson Raphaelson (based on *Birthdays*, a play by Laszlo Bus-Fekete) 1934, 20th Century Fox. www.lubitsch.com/heaven.html.

36. *The Horn Blows at Midnight*, director Raoul Walsh, writers Sam Hellman and James V. Kern, 1945, Warner Brothers.

37. *The Lift*, director and writer Jason Allen, UCLA Short Fiction Program 2000, www.thelift.org/thefilm.htm.

38. Rolf Becker, *Nocturno 1951*, Berlin/Frankfurt:Suhrkamp, 1951, p. 196f, quoted in Gruber, "The Yankee Loves the Lift," p. 102.

39. Colson Whitehead, *The Intuitionist*, p. 46, p. 16. On the symbolism of trains in early film see Lynne Kirby, *Parallel Tracks: The Railroad and Silent Cinema*, Durham, North Carolina (Duke University Press) 1997.

40. Maude Hutchins, "The Elevator," *The Elevator, Stories*, New York (Morrow) 1962, pp. 1–38.

41. Hutchins, *The Elevator*, p. 3.

42. Hutchins, *The Elevator*, p. 25.

43. Yvonne Rainer, "MURDER and murder," The *Performing Arts Journal*, 19.1, 1997, pp. 76–117.

44. *Sliding Doors*, director and writer Peter Howitt, 1998, Miramax Films/Paramount Pictures.

45. *Monsters, Inc.*, directors Pete Docter et al., writers Robert L. Baird et al., 2001, Pixar Animation Studios/Walt Disney Pictures.

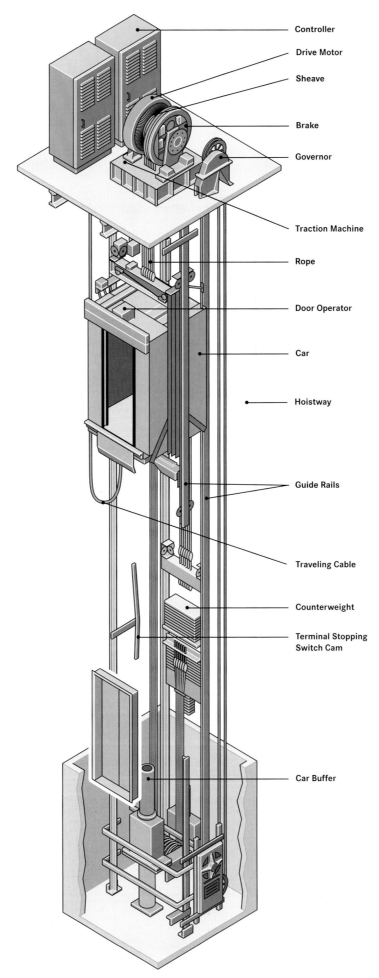

Controller

Drive Motor

Sheave

Brake

Governor

Traction Machine

Rope

Door Operator

Car

Hoistway

Guide Rails

Traveling Cable

Counterweight

Terminal Stopping
Switch Cam

Car Buffer

Diagram of an electric gearless elevator, 1997.

Glossary

Richard Evans

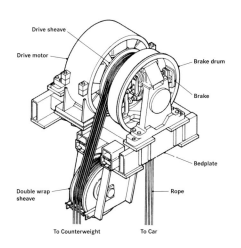

A double-wrap gearless machine. From George R. Strakosch, ed., *The Vertical Transportation Handbook*, 3rd edn New York (John Wiley & Sons, Inc.) 1998.

A double-deck elevator in the Cities Service Building, New York, designed by Clinton & Russell, 1932.

Balustrade The side of an escalator extending above the steps.

Brake An electro-mechanical device used to prevent the elevator from moving when the car is at rest and no power is applied to the hoist motor.

Buffer A piston or spring device for absorbing the impact of a descending elevator car or counterweight at the extreme lower limit of travel.

Car (elevator) The load-carrying unit, sometimes called the cab.

Controller An electrical device that controls all the movements of an elevator, such as answering calls, taking passengers to their requested floors, and opening and closing the doors. Controllers have evolved from simple electric mechanisms to sophisticated computers capable of smarter dispatching and overseeing safety components.

Counterweight A weight that counterbalances the weight of an elevator car plus approximately 40% of the capacity load.

Door Operator A motor-driven device mounted on the car that opens and closes the car and shaft doors.

Double-Deck Elevator An approach to reducing the space required for elevators in taller buildings by having a car with two compartments. The upper and lower decks are loaded simultaneously, with passengers destined for odd-numbered floors entering the bottom deck and those for the even-numbered floors entering the upper deck.

Dumbwaiter A small elevator used to move material (not people) and operated from the landing, and not within the cab. Originally hand operated, most dumbwaiters today are electrically powered.

Electric Elevator An electrically powered traction machine that raises and lowers the car on steel ropes. The ropes are looped around sheaves (grooved pulleys), one end is attached to the car and one is attached to a counterweight that offsets the weight of the elevator car. When a passenger pushes a button to select a floor, the electric motor is started through a controller to turn the sheave and thus propel the car to a floor. The controller, the brain of the system, slows the car and with the aid of the terminal stopping switch cam stops it at the selected floor and opens the doors. The controller also senses when a person requests an elevator from a floor and schedules a stop to pick up the requestor.

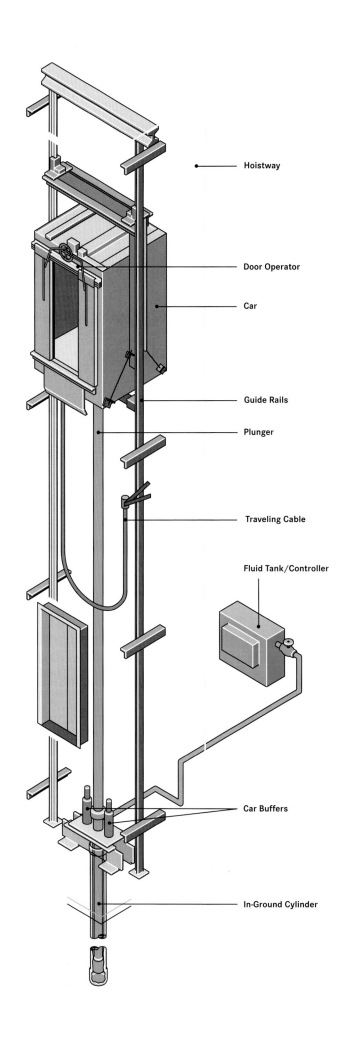

Hoistway

Door Operator

Car

Guide Rails

Plunger

Traveling Cable

Fluid Tank/Controller

Car Buffers

In-Ground Cylinder

Diagram of a holed hydraulic elevator, 1997.

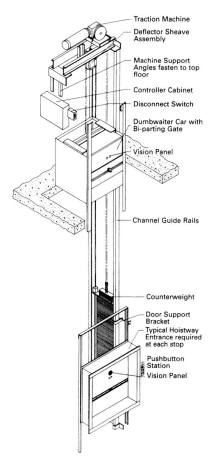

The "Ambassador TR Dumbwaiter," 1995. From George R. Strakosch, ed., *The Vertical Transportation Handbook*, 3rd edn New York (John Wiley & Sons, Inc.) 1998.

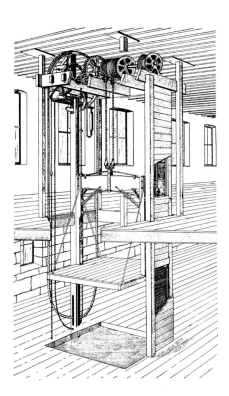

A hand elevator designed by John H. Hallings, *c.* 1919. From John H. Jallings, *Elevators*, Chicago (American Technical Society) 1919; reprinted by *Elevator World*, Inc., Mobile, Alabama, 1995.

Elevatoring The technique of applying available elevator technology to satisfy the demand of a particular installation. It considers such factors as number of floors, population of floors, and use of the building.

Escalator A moving stairway connecting upper and lower landings. A truss or rigid structure bridges the space between the landings supporting the escalator's steps, balustrade, and handrail. A track is built into the truss to guide the steps, which are pulled along by a chain powered by an electric motor. The moving handrail is similarly powered by the electric motor.

Governor A mechanical speed-monitoring and controlling device used with both elevators and escalators to slow or stop them if overspeed occurs.

Guide Rails Vertical steel tracks that stabilize and guide the travel of an elevator car or counterweight.

Human Interface The devices that make it possible for an elevator rider to operate the elevator mechanism. Elevator operators are seldom found today, so passengers operate the elevators themselves; there are many devices that make that possible. About the only direct action a passenger makes is to call an elevator from a landing and then select a floor after boarding. However, there are many other interfaces that the rider may observe or utilize when necessary. Lights and indicators register the requests and show floor numbers, directions, and arrivals. Sound may also be used. Door protection, emergency lights, and communications are there for emergencies. All of these features are overseen by an electric controller.

Hand Elevator A lifting device propelled by human force, pulling on a rope or turning a wheel. The operator may be on the elevator platform or on a floor. The figure shows gears and pulleys that give a mechanical advantage when winding a rope on a drum to lift the elevator. This type of device was common in factories and warehouses for moving material between floors.

Hoistway (or elevator shaft) A vertical enclosed space for the travel of one or more elevators, and their counterweights.

Hydraulic Elevator An elevator that uses fluid under pressure to push the car up. Early hydraulic elevators used city water pressure controlled by an operator in the car tugging on a rope that opened or closed a valve. Today hydraulic elevators are installed in buildings from two to six stories high and other low-rise installations. When a passenger pushes a button to select a floor, the controller registers the request and causes an electric motor to pump hydraulic fluid into a cylinder to raise the car to the selected floor. The direct-plunger type (shown opposite) requires a cylinder extending downward into the ground of a length equal to the height of the elevator rise. Earlier arrangements, now generally obsolete, were developed using ropes, sheaves, and vertical or horizontal above-ground cylinders to eliminate the need for the deep hole.

Interlock A device on each hoistway door that mechanically locks the door shut and signals to the controller that the car may move.

Lift The British term for an elevator.

Paternoster A European device with cars running continuously up and down in adjacent hoistways. Its use requires agility on the part of passengers, who step on to the moving car (cab) and step off on their desired floor. From the Latin phrase meaning "our father."

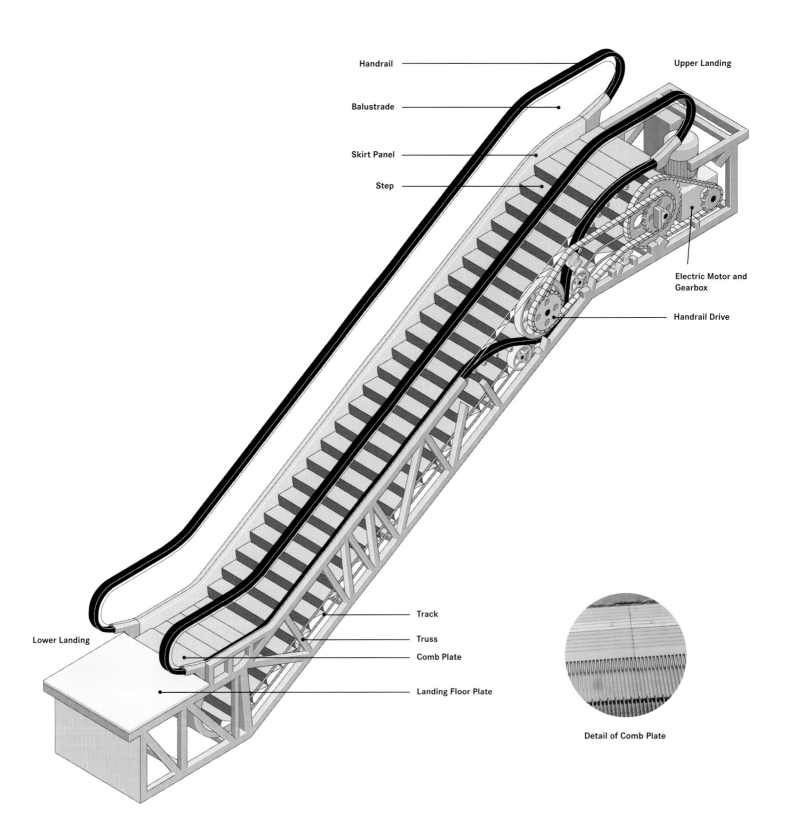

Handrail

Upper Landing

Balustrade

Skirt Panel

Step

Electric Motor and
Gearbox

Handrail Drive

Track

Truss

Comb Plate

Lower Landing

Landing Floor Plate

Detail of Comb Plate

Diagram of an escalator, 2000.

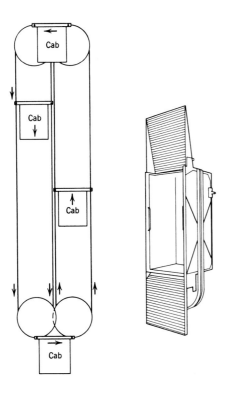

A paternoster elevator. From George R. Strakosch, ed., *The Vertical Transportation Handbook*, 3rd edn New York (John Wiley & Sons, Inc.) 1998.

A steam-powered belt-driven elevator, *c.* 1868.

Rise The vertical distance traversed by an elevator car from the lowest to the highest landing, or as applied to escalators, the height of a stair step or flight of stairs.

Rope (or hoist rope) A twisted, multi-strand steel cable that passes over the drive sheave and supports and lifts the car and counterweight.

Safety Components The many features the rider does not see that make elevators safe to ride. The governor and rope brake sense overspeed and can safely stop the car. Limit switches in the hoistway stop the car if it travels too far at the top or bottom of the shaft. Each rope is capable of supporting five times the maximum load of the elevator, and a minimum of three ropes provide further redundancy. Car and counterweight buffers act as shock absorbers if those units go below their normal lower limits. Safety edges protruding from the leading end of a door panel or electronic "eyes" sense if anyone is in the path of the door and cause it to reopen. The controller in the machine room processes all the electrical signals initiated by the passengers and assures that doors are closed and locked before a car can run, that power is sufficient, and that no overload exists.

Sheave A wheel mounted in bearings and having one or more grooves over which a rope or ropes may pass. Commonly but incorrectly pronounced "shiv."

Steam-powered Belt-driven Elevator In the nineteenth century steam engines were commonly used to drive elevators by means of leather belts or worm gearing. Factories and mills often had rotating shafts powered by a central prime mover to drive the production machinery. This could be connected to the winding drum of the elevator. By tugging on a rope that ran through the car, the operator could control the elevator.

Traction Elevator The simplest and most efficient form of electric elevator, and the only one capable of almost limitless rise. Consists of an electric motor, a sheave, and a brake all on a common shaft (see image on p. 197). The motor turns the sheave and friction between the hoist ropes and the sheave moves the car. The car and counterweight are at opposite ends of the hoist ropes.

Traveling Cable A cable that provides electrical connection between an elevator car and a connection at the midpoint of the hoistway. This cable provides power for lights and the door motors and carries the signals to and from the controller.

A gearless machine with flyball and governor, developed by Ove Arup & Partners, 1999.

A sectional perspective of a single worm-geared machine developed by Ove Arup & Partners, 1999.

An elevator car frame, developed by Ove Arup & Partners, 1999.

A typical overhead sheave arrangement, developed by Ove Arup & Partners, 1999.

Statistics

Richard Evans

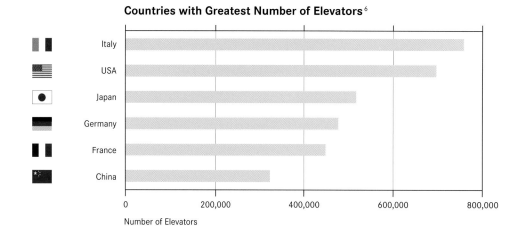

Countries with Greatest Number of Elevators [6]

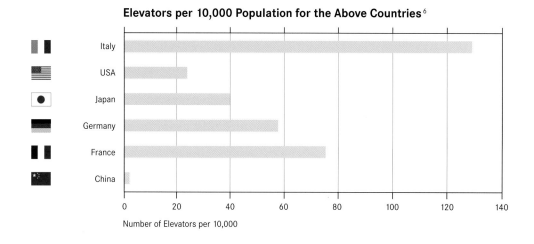

Elevators per 10,000 Population for the Above Countries [6]

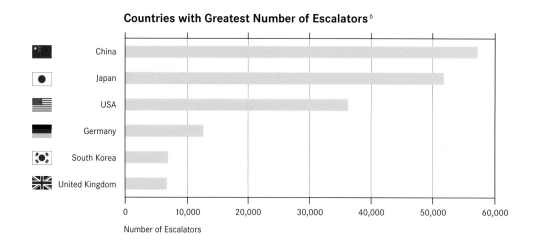

Countries with Greatest Number of Escalators [6]

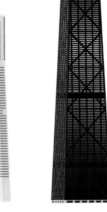

Taipei Financial Center
Fastest Modern Electric
Taiwan
Completed 2003
1667 ft (508.1 m)
61 Elevators

John Hancock Center
Typical Modern Electric
Chicago
Completed 1969
1131 ft (344.7 m)
50 Elevators

Washington Metro
Modern Hydraulic
Washington, D.C.
Completed 2001
165 Hydraulic
40 Others

Yokohama Landmark Tower
Second Fastest Modern Electric
Japan
Completed 1993
972 ft (296.3 m)
59 Elevators

Singer Building
Early Electric
New York
Completed 1908
672 ft (204.8 m)
15 Elevators

Washington Monument
Early Steam-Powered[†]
Washington, D.C.
Completed 1888
555 ft (169.2 m)
1 Elevator

Elevator Speeds in Some Well-Known Installations [1,6]

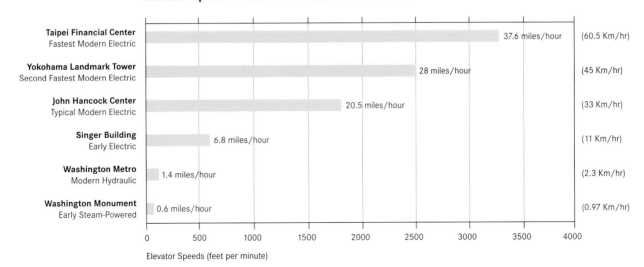

Elevator Speeds (feet per minute)

[†] In 2001 an electric elevator was installed in the Washington Monument that runs at 500 feet per minute (2.54 m/second) but can be slowed to 150 feet per minute (0.76 m/second), giving visitors the chance to view inscribed stones through the transparent elevator walls.

A diagram of elevator traffic in the Prudential Building, Chicago, 2000. Drawing by Alicia Yin Cheng, adapted from an Otis Elevator Company advertisement of 1954.

Modern office buildings require efficient vertical circulation. This graph charts the daily traffic pattern in the Prudential Building, where 27 automatic elevators completed an estimated 60,000 passenger rides every day.

UP traffic

DOWN traffic

8:30 9:00 9:30 10:00 10:30 11:00 12:00 12:30 1:00 1:30 2:00 2:30 3:00 3:30 4:00 4:30 5:00 5:30

Moving Walkway Speeds [2,3,4,5,6]

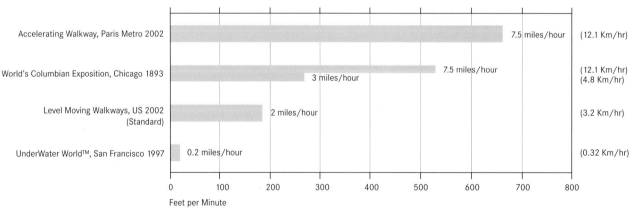

Accelerating Walkway, Paris Metro 2002	7.5 miles/hour	(12.1 Km/hr)
World's Columbian Exposition, Chicago 1893	7.5 miles/hour / 3 miles/hour	(12.1 Km/hr) / (4.8 Km/hr)
Level Moving Walkways, US 2002 (Standard)	2 miles/hour	(3.2 Km/hr)
UnderWater World™, San Francisco 1997	0.2 miles/hour	(0.32 Km/hr)

0   100   200   300   400   500   600   700   800

Feet per Minute

1. James W. Fortune, "Taipei Financial Center," *Elevator World*, October 2002, p. 52.

Robert L. Seymour and Tony Maglietta, "Washington Monument Renovation: A Project and Its History," *Elevator World*, January 1999, p. 61.

Ernest Flagg, "The Singer Building, New York," *Architects' and Builders' Magazine*, vol. 9, no. 10, July 1908, pp. 429–44.

2. PROAVIA (French Trade Association for Airport Equipment and Consultants and Air Navigation) website http://www.proavia.com/members/cnim/acti.htm.

3. James W. Shepp and Daniel B. Shepp, *Shepp's World's Fair Photographed*, Chicago (Globe Bible Publishing Co.) 1893, p. 322.

4. George R. Strakosch, ed., *The Vertical Transportation Handbook*, 3rd edn New York (John Wiley & Sons, Inc.) 1998, p. 3.

5. Johnathan L. Butler, "Two Firsts for San Francisco: A Curved Moving Walk and an UnderWater World™," *Elevator World*, February 1997, p. 38.

6. All data taken from the *The Elevator World Source 2001–2002*, published by *Elevator World* magazine in October 2001. The data was collected through a network of correspondents, contacts, subscribers, and elevator industry associates. Most of the information dates to the year 2000. Data was unavailable for some countries (i.e. Sweden, Russia, Spain, etc.). There are no official reporting bodies, so all data should be considered approximate. Statistics listing the total number of elevators in each country include existing and new installations, but in some cases also include moving sidewalks. The statistics for China do not include Hong Kong. For more information on methods of gathering industry data, see *The Elevator World Source 2001-2002*, vol. 49, no. 10, Mobile, Alabama (Elevator World, Inc.) pp. 425–95.

Contributors

Keller Easterling is an architect, writer, and associate professor of Architecture at Yale University. She is the author of *Organization Space: Landscapes, Highways, and Houses in America* (1999), and numerous journal articles. Bridging the gap between architecture and infrastructure, Easterling views architecture as part of an ecology of interrelationships and linkages, and she treats the expression of organizational character as part of the architectural endeavor. She is also co-author of *Call it Home* (1992), a laserdisc history of American suburbia from 1934–60, and author of *American Town Plans* (1993). She is currently working on a book entitled *Terra Incognita* about spatial products in pivotal political locations around the world.

Susan Garfinkel earned her Ph.D. in American Civilization from the University of Pennsylvania in 1997. She is currently a research specialist with the Digital Reference Team at the Library of Congress, Washington, D.C., and is affiliated with the Department of American Studies, University of Maryland, College Park. Among her areas of special interest are American material and visual culture, vernacular architecture, popular art, science fiction, gender and technology, and narrative forms. She has written extensively on the cultural history of the American built environment in both the eighteenth and the twentieth centuries.

Alisa Goetz, co-curator and editor, is an assistant curator at the National Building Museum. Her previous exhibitions at the museum include *Tools as Art VI: Instruments of Change (The Hechinger Collection)* (2000); *Monuments & Memory: Washington, D.C. Architects Explore the Language of Monuments* (2001–02); *From Arts and Crafts to Modern Design: The Architecture of William L. Price* (2001–02); *Zaha Hadid Laboratory* (2002); and *Saving Mount Vernon: The Birth of Preservation in America* (2003).

Peter A. Hall is a journalist and design critic based in New York. He is a contributing writer for *Metropolis* magazine and the senior editor at the Design Institute, University of Minnesota, where he is developing a book on mapping and an online journal. He also teaches a seminar on design theory at Yale School of Art's MFA graphic design program. He has written widely about design in its various forms—from TV graphics and neon lights to bridges and spaceships—for publications including *I.D.* magazine, *Eye*, *The Guardian,* and *Print*. He wrote and co-edited the books *Tibor Kalman: Perverse Optimist* (2000) and *Sagmeister: Made You Look* (2001) and co-authored *Pause: 59 Minutes of Motion Graphics* (2000).

John King is the urban design writer for the *San Francisco Chronicle*, a position he created in 2001. His pieces examine and critique the built environment, with a focus on how architecture, planning, and development shape life today. He was made a finalist in the criticism category by the Pulitzer Prize committee, received a special commendation from the California Council, and won the President's Prize from the California chapter of the American Institute of Architects for creating a deeper awareness of design issues among readers. In 2002 he began writing on architectural issues for *Metropolis* and *Boston Architecture*; he also wrote the introduction to *Marcel Sedletzky: Architect and Teacher* (2002).

Phil Patton is the author of several books, including *Made in USA: The Secret Histories of the Things that Made America* (1992), *Dreamland* (1998), and *Bug: The Strange Mutations of the World's Most Famous Automobile* (2002). A contributing editor to *I.D.* magazine, *Esquire*, and *Wired*, he also writes frequently about design and technology for the *New York Times*. Phil Patton was consulting curator for the 1999 exhibition *Different Roads: Automobiles for the Next Century* at the Museum of Modern Art, New York.

Julie Wosk is a professor of art history, English, and studio painting at the State University of New York, Maritime College. She has written extensively on technology, design, and art, including the books *Breaking Frame: Technology and the Visual Arts in the Nineteenth Century* (1992) and *Women and the Machine: Representations From the Spinning Wheel to the Electronic Age* (2001). Her articles on art and technology, literature, and design have appeared in *Design Issues, Technology Review, Technology And Culture, Art And Artists, Leonardo*, and elsewhere. She is also a painter and photographer whose works have been exhibited in New York and Connecticut and reviewed in the *New York Times*.

Acknowledgments

This book, to accompany the exhibition *Up, Down, Across: Elevators, Escalators, and Moving Sidewalks*, is the result of collaboration with many individuals and organizations, and we would like to take this opportunity to recognize them.

First we wish to thank our sponsors United Technologies Corporation and Otis Elevator Company for making this project possible. *Up, Down, Across* began as a way to celebrate the 150th anniversary of Elisha Otis's presentation of the safety brake at the 1853–54 New York Exposition. It has evolved into an appreciation of that event, and how what followed has impacted on the way we work, live, and spend our leisure time. For her ability to get this project off the ground the exhibition team would like to thank Marie Dalton-Meyer.

The *Up, Down, Across* team thanks the authors of the six essays—Keller Easterling, Susan Garfinkel, Peter A. Hall, John King, Phil Patton, and Julie Wosk—for helping create one of the first books to evaluate the role of conveyance devices on architecture and culture. We also thank Dr. Henry Petroski for his insightful preface on the origins and workings of elevators, escalators, and moving sidewalks.

Several people also deserve thanks for their roles as advisors to this project. Firstly, Dr. Lee E. Gray, Associate Professor of Architecture at the University of North Carolina, Charlotte, who negotiated a busy schedule to discuss the history of elevators and evaluate the photo essays. Secondly, Robert M. Vogel, Curator Emeritus of the Smithsonian Institution, who edited the technical information in this book and has been enormously helpful in general. Thirdly, Robert S. Caporale, Editor of *Elevator World* magazine, and his staff, for informing their subscribers about *Up, Down, Across* and providing our team with a link to the conveyance industry. Fourth, to David Gissen, Assistant Professor of Architecture at Pennsylvania State University, who established the look and feel for this project with his early proposal.

Of course this project would not exist without the extensive research that went into it. For giving us access to the National Association of Elevator Contractors' 53rd Annual Convention and World Elevator Expo II we give thanks to Theresa Shirley and her colleagues at NAEC. It was a wonderful opportunity to meet industry representatives and get a look at the latest trends for elevators, escalators, dumb waiters, automatic garages, and a whole host of other devices.

Grateful appreciation to the numerous institutions, organizations, companies, and individuals who also assisted us in locating images: Advanced Transport Systems Ltd.; Alfred Englert; Andrea Gibbs at the National Gallery of Art, Washington, D.C.; Andrea Haussmann at MK Automation Engineering, Inc.; Artifice, Inc.; Baltimore Streetcar Museum Inc.; Barbara Hooven at Cannon

Design; Beatriz Valiente at Photononstop; Bernd Dahlmann, California State University Fresno; Cayce Blanchard, Greg Jones, and Kevin Hamilton at Mitsubishi Electric Corporation; Chris Smidt at Wildeck, Inc.; Cindy Cheung at Hong Kong Air Terminals Limited; CORBIS; Craig Swank at Swisslog; David Barron; David Liu; David Strettell at Magnum Photos; Deborah Sorensen; Dominique Gapany at Real Intercontinental Metrocentro Managua; Donna Shipman at the Port of Long Beach; Dylan Leblanc at Skyscraperpage.com; Francis Toussaint; FROG Navigation Systems; General Motors Media Archives; Getty Images, Inc.; Gina Gayle; GreatBuildings.com; Hanna-Barbera Productions Inc.; Hillwood Development Corporation; Hugh Robertson at London's Transport Museum; Jacqueline A. Miney and Stephanie Graf at Schindler Elevator Corporation; James W. Fortune and Bryan R. Hines at Lerch, Bates & Associates; Jeffery Howe; John Bigay at Captivate Network, Inc.; John Wiley & Sons, Inc.; Joyce Dutton at Six Flags Astroworld; Katherine Swope and Alicia Wilson at John Portman & Associates; Kathleen Moenster at the Jefferson National Expansion Memorial; Lee Gray; Library of Congress; Lou Di Gennaro at the Avery Architectural & Fine Arts Library at Columbia University; Berthold Pesch at Stephan Braunfels Architekten; MGM; Marguerite Lavin at the Museum of the City of New York; Martin Lowson at ULTra (University of Bristol); Matot, Inc.; Michael Decker at Diller + Scofidio; Michael Goodman; Michael Neff at Maersk, Inc.; Michele Aldrich and Debbie Sifuentes at Otis Elevator Company; Museum of History & Industry, Seattle; Norman McGrath; Nouvelles Editions de Films; OMA/ Rem Koolhaas; Paramount Pictures; Paul Wirtz; Phil Patton; Pflow Industries, Inc.; Richard Evans; San Diego Historical Society; Sebastian Wormell at Harrods Limited; Bob Worthington in the Division of the History of Technology, National Museum of American History, Smithsonian Institution; Stacie Hyman and David Clothier at *Elevator World* magazine; Tivoli Gardens; T.L. Jones, Limited; United States Patent and Trademark Office; Universal Pictures; the University of Maryland; the University of Texas; and Warner Brothers.

For the graphic design of this book and exhibition, and guest curation of the exhibition, thanks are due to Pentagram Design, Inc. partner Abbott Miller. He has been ably assisted by his associates James Hicks, Jeremy Hoffman, and Jess Mackta. Their work has given this subject-matter the flair and excitement with which it is not usually associated. This book is published in partnership with Merrell Publishers, and we would like to thank editorial director Julian Honer, managing editor Anthea Snow, editor Sam Wythe and design manager Kate Ward for their excellent work.

At the National Building Museum we are grateful for the work and support of our many colleagues. Susan Henshaw Jones, former president of the National Building Museum, enthusiastically endorsed this project during her tenure. Howard Decker, Chief Curator, participated in the early conception of the project and has provided consistent support of the exhibition and catalog. Catherine Crane Frankel, Director of Exhibitions, has managed much of the logistics for the exhibition, keeping us within the budget and on schedule. Chrysanthe Broikos, Curator, shared her experience in creating exhibition catalogs, carefully reviewed this material, and provided support above and beyond what was expected, for which I am grateful. Martin Moeller, Senior Vice President for Special Projects, reviewed the catalog material and provided helpful comments during exhibition planning. Essence Newhoff, Director of Development for Exhibitions, worked on the project from the beginning and has coordinated the effort between our sponsors and the Museum. Deborah Sorensen, Exhibitions Assistant, has ably handled many of the administrative tasks associated with producing the catalog and exhibition. Ed Worthy, Vice President for Education, provided helpful comments during planning of the exhibition and, with Michelle Rinehart, Director of Public

Programs, and Jaime Lawson, Public Programs Coordinator, developed the lectures and other public programs. Ayumu Ota, Scout and Family Programs Coordinator, created engaging programs for children based on the exhibition. Dana Twersky, Collections Manager, and Cecelia Gibson, Exhibitions Registrar, coordinated the loan and donation of objects large and small. Hank Griffith, Exhibitions Coordinator, with Christopher Maclay, Exhibitions Preparator, and Elizabeth Kaleida, Exhibitions Designer and Preparator, made considerable contributions to the exhibition's design, fabrication, and installation. Don Holstrom, Systems Administrator, greatly eased the transmission of images via an FTP site. Dedicated National Building Museum volunteer Richard Evans not only provided the glossary and statistics appendices, but also spent countless hours researching, and providing technical and editorial support. His contributions to this project have been invaluable. We would also like to thank volunteer Ann Lange, interns Trisha Van Wagner, Emily Farmer, and Erin Alane Carlson for their eager assistance.

We would also be amiss not to mention our peers and friends, including Ramee Gentry and Mary Konsoulis, for their counsel and suggestions.

Alisa Goetz
Assistant Curator
National Building Museum

Bibliography

F.A. Annett, "Automatic Dispatching Improves Elevator Service," *Power*, June 24, 1930, pp. 986–87

F.A. Annett, *Electric Elevators*, New York (McGraw Hill Co.) 1935; Reprinted by Elevator World, Mobile, Alabama in 1989 under title of *Elevators, Electric and Electrohydraulic Elevators, Escalators, Moving Walks and Ramps*

"Automated Elevator Control," *Building Operating Management*, July 1990

"Automatic Elevators for Apartment Houses," *American Architect*, vol. 129, no. 2499, June 20, 1926, pp. 633–36

Reyner Banham, "The Great Gizmo," *Design 12*, September 1965

Marius Bar and José de Olivares, *The Parisian Dream City: A Portfolio of Photographic Views of the World's Exposition at Paris*, St. Louis (N.D. Thompson) 1900

G.C. Barney, ed., *Elevator Abstracts Including Escalators*, Chichester, UK (Ellis Horwood) 1990

G.C. Barney, ed., *Elevator Technology*, Papers of the International Conference on Elevator Technologies, Chichester, UK (Ellis Horwood) 1986–

G.C. Barney and A.G. Loher, *Elevator Electric Drives: Concepts and Principles, Controls and Practice*, London (Ellis Horwood) 1990

William Baxter, "The Electric Elevator Versus the Hydraulic Elevator," *Engineering Magazine*, II, April/September 1896, pp. 478–85

Jack Bechdolt, *Going Up: The Story of Vertical Transportation*, Abingdon Press, 1948

Michael J. Bedner, *Interior Pedestrian Places*, New York (Whitney Library of Design) 1989

Umberto Boccioni, Carlo D. Carrà et al., "Technical Manifesto," April 11, 1910, in *Futurist Manifestos*, ed. Embro Apollonio, trans. Robert Brain, New York (Viking Press) 1973

Robert M. Boggs, "Motion Control: It's More Advanced Than Ever," *Design News*, September 18, 1989, pp. 98–99

R.P. Bolton, "Defective and Dangerous Features in Elevator Operation," *The Engineering Magazine*, 1905, pp. 737–40

F.P. Boone and S.W. Palmer, "The Modern Passenger Elevator," *National Engineer*, vol. 19, April 1915, pp. 187–88

Edgar M. Bouton, "Variable Voltage Control as Applied to Electric Elevators," *A.I.I.E. Transactions*, 1924, pp. 199–219

Andrea Branzi, "Mass Creativity," *The Hot House: Italian New Wave Design*, Cambridge, Massachusetts (MIT Press) 1984

Andrea Branzi, "No-Stop City, Residential Parking, Climatic Universal System," *Domus*, no. 496, March 1971

A.E. Brooke, "The Fraser Electric Elevator," *Association of Engineering Societies Transactions*, August 1898, pp. 93–111

Thomas E. Brown, "Passenger Elevators," *American Society of Civil Engineers Transactions*, no. 22, presented at International Engineering Congress, 1904, pp. 132–204

"Building Engineering: Operatorless Elevators," *Architectural Forum*, vol. 98, sec. III, January 1953, pp. 154–55

Donald J. Bush and Richard Guy Wilson, *The Streamlined Decade*, New York (George Braziller) 1975

Arianna Callocchi, "Lifts as an Expression of Architecture," *Elevator World*, May 2001

Charles Carrol, "Apartment-Houses," *Appleton's Journal*, vol. 5, no. 6, December 1878, pp. 529–35

Arthur Chandler, "Culmination: The Paris Exposition Universelle of 1900," in *World's Fair Magazine*, vol. 7, no. 3, 1987

John Cheever, "Christmas is a Sad Season for the Poor," *The Stories of John Cheever*, New York (Knopf) 1978, pp. 128–36

Xiangming Chen, "The Evolution of Free Economic Zones and the Recent Development of Cross-National Growth Zones," *International Journal of Urban and Regional Research*, vol. 19, no. 4, 1995

Sheldon Cheney and Martha Candler Cheney, *Art and the Machine: An Account of Industrial Design in 20th Century America*, New York (McGraw Hill) 1936

Kyle E. Ciani and Cynthia Malinick, "From Spanish Romance to Neon Confidence and Demolition Fear: The Twentieth-Century Life of the El Cortez Hotel," *The Journal of San Diego History*, vol. 46, no. 1, winter 2000

George R. Collins, *Visionary Drawings of Architecture and Planning: 20th Century Through the 1980s*, Cambridge, Massachusetts (MIT Press) 1979

David A. Cooper, "The History of the Escalator," *Lift Report*, January/February 2000

Joseph J. Corn and Brian Horrigan, *Yesterday's Tomorrows: Past Visions Of The American Future*, New York (Summit Books) 1984

Russell G. and Walter M. Cory with Yasuo Matsui, "The Starrett-Lehigh Building, New York, N.Y.," *Architectural Forum*, vol. 55, October 1931

Russell G. and Walter M. Cory with Yasuo Matsui, "The Starrett-Lehigh Building, New York, N.Y.," *Architectural Record*, vol. 71, January 1932, pp. 30–35

"The Dangers of Elevator Travel," *Literary Digest*, 29:20, November, 12, 1904, p. 696

A.C. David, "A Co-operative Studio Building," *Architectural Record*, October 1903, pp. 233–54

Robert L. Davison, "Procedure in Designing a Theater," *Architectural Record*, vol. 67, May 1930, pp. 457–96

"The Development of Elevators," *Universal Engineering*, vol. 63, no. 6, June 1936, pp. 27–29

John Morris Dixon, "Thirty-Story Slab of Ingenuity," *Architectural Forum*, September 1970, pp. 20–27

"Double-Deck Lifts Ready in City Soon," *New York Times*, October 18, 1931, pp. 5–6

Sharon Cramer Drain, "A Mechanic Gave the World a Lift," *American History*, November 1987, pp. 42–46, 50

Dynamic City, Milan (Fondation Pour L'Architecture, Skira) 2000

Barrett Eastman and Frédéric Mayer, *Paris, 1900: The American Guide to City and Exposition*, New York (Baldwin & Eastman) 1899

"Electric Elevators," *Electrical World*, April 3, 1897, pp. 447–50

"Electric Elevators," *Electrical World*, April 10, 1897, pp. 475–76

"Electric Elevators," *Electrical World*, April 17, 1897, pp. 506–07

"Electric Elevators," *Electrical World*, April 24, 1897, pp. 530–34

"Electronic Lifts," *New York Times*, April 7, 1949

"Electronics Applied to Elevator Systems," *New York Times*, June 15, 1948, p. 29

"Elevator Disease," *Literary Digest*, 20:2, June 9, 1900, p. 698

"Elevator Dispatching by Telephone," *Electrical Review and Western Electrician*, vol. 65, no. 16, October 17, 1914, pp. 751–53

"Elevator Economics," *Architectural Forum*, vol. 100, May 1954, pp. 178–79

"The Elevator Equipment of the Singer Building," *Owners and Builders Magazine*, September 1907, p. 27

"Elevator Problems in Lofty Tower," *New York Times*, April 1, 1908, p. 5

"Elevator World Educational Package and Reference Library," I, "Elevator Control and Operation," II, "Elevator Maintenance and Traffic," III, "Construction Performance and Hydraulics," compilation of articles from *Elevator World*, Mobile, Alabama

"Elevators to be Speeded," *New York Times*, June 16, 1931, p. 30

Cecil D. Elliott, *Techniques and Architecture: The Development of Materials and Systems for Building*, Cambridge, Massachusetts (MIT Press) 1992

Kerstin Englert and Alfred Englert, *Lifts in Berlin: 100 Years of History*, Berlin (Jovis) 1998

"Fast Elevators Planned," *New York Times* (Real Estate Section) March 8, 1931, p. 4

"First Dual Elevator Run Successfully," *New York Times* (Business Opportunities Section) January 19, 1931, p. 48

"The Escalator or Continuous Elevator," *Engineering*, vol. 70, November 30, 1900, pp. 699–700

Andrea Fisher, *Let Us Now Praise Famous Women: American Women Photographers for the U.S. Government, 1935–44*, London (Pandora) 1987

Thomas Fisher, "Spiral Escalators," *Progressive Architecture*, July 1985, p. 137

John Cushman Fistere, "Pneumatic Tube Systems," *Architectural Forum*, November 1931

Rodney Fitch and Lance Knobel, *Retail Design*, New York (Whitney Library of Design) 1990

Valerie Fletcher, *Dreams and Nightmares: Utopian Visions in Modern Art*, Washington, D.C. (Smithsonian Institution Press) 1983

Fred C. Floyd, "Modern Elevators," *Architecture and Building*, January 28–29, 1898, pp. 39–41

"For Otis: More Electronics," *Business Week*, October 17, 1953, pp. 119–20

Barbara Ford, *The Elevator*, New York (Walker & Company) 1982

J.W. Fortune, "Revolutionary Lift Designs for Mega-High-Rise Buildings," *Elevator World*, April 1998

T. Fukuda, "AC Feedback Control in Japan," *Elevator World*, May 1978, August 1978, and January 1979.

Paul Gapp, "Oh Boy, O'Hare! At United's Terminal, Getting There is Half the Fun," *Chicago Tribune*, October 4, 1987

Glenn Garvin, "Mall Escalators Delight, Terrify Nicaraguans," *Austin American-Statesman*, February 15, 1999

Jean Gavois, *Going Up: An Informal History of the Elevator from the Pyramids to the Present*, Connecticut (Otis Elevator Company) 1983

Emerson Goble, ed., "Mail Conveyers in High-Rise Buildings," *Architectural Record*, October 1965, p. 209

Hilda G. Golden, "Urbanization and Cities," Lexington, Massachusetts (D.C. Heath & Co.) 1981

Les Gould, "Free-ranging AGVs Cover 100,000-sq-ft Assembly Area," *Modern Materials Handling*, December 1994

Stephen Graham and Simon Marvin, *Splintering Urbanism: Networked Infrastructures, Technological Mobilities and the Urban Condition*, London (Routledge) 2001

Graham, Anderson, Probst & White, "Merchandise Mart Building, Chicago, Ill.," *American Architect*, vol. 133, June 20, 1928, p. 486

"Great Northern, Piccadilly, and Brompton Railway," *The Engineer*, December 14, 1906, p. 598

G.B. Gusrae, "Moving Stairways for Tall Buildings: They cost less ... and take less space," *Architectural Record*, April 1952, pp. 213–17

Joseph Harriss, *The Tallest Tower: Eiffel and the Belle Epoque*, Washington, D.C. (Regnery Gateway) 1989

Martin Healey, "Variable Speed Drives," *Instrument and Control Engineering*, April 1967, pp. 36–40

Lajos Héder with Ellen Shoshkes, *Aesthetics in Transportation*, Washington, D.C. (U.S. Department of Transportation) 1980

Robert Hendrickson, *The Grand Emporiums: Illustrated History of America's Great Department Stores*, New York (Stein and Day) 1979

Phil Hirsch, "Revolution in Vertical Transportation," *American Business*, vol. 24, October 1954, pp. 20, 21, 40

Elizabeth S. Holdame and G.R.T. Ross, *The Philosophical Works of Descartes*, I–II, New York (Dover Publications) 1955

R.H. Hollier and L.F. Gelders, eds., "Automated Handling of Intermodal Containers With AGVs," *Automated Guided Vehicle Systems, Proceedings of the 6th International Conference*, 1988

Albert A. Hopkins, "Elevators with Electric Brains," *Scientific American*, October 1925, pp. 249–50

C.A. Houghtaling, "The Security Storage Warehouse, Portland, Ore.," *Architectural Record*, vol. 67, 1930, p. 511

Edwin J. Houston, *Electricity in Every-Day Life,* II, New York (P.F. Collier) 1905

Edward Hungerford, *The Romance of a Great Store*, New York (R.M. McBride) 1922

F.O. Hunt, "Electrically Driven Lifts," *The Electrical Engineer*, April 7, 1905, pp. 489–90

Maude Hutchins, "The Elevator," *The Elevator, Stories*, New York (Morrow) 1962, pp. 1–38

F. Hymans, *Electric Elevators, Book 1; Electric Traction Elevators, Book 2; Electric Elevator Operation*, Scranton, Pennsylvania (International Textbook Press) 1931

"In Search of the Past: A History of the Elevator Industry," *Elevator World*, Mobile, Alabama, publication date unknown

John Inglis, "Evolution of Safety Gears," *Elevator World*, April 2000

International Library of Technology, *Elevators*, Scranton, Pennsylvania (International Textbook Company) 1902

Donald Dale Jackson, "Elevating Thoughts From Elisha Otis and Fellow Uplifters," *Smithsonian Magazine*, November 1989

John H. Jallings, *Elevators: A Practical Treatise on the Development and Design of Hand, Belt, Steam, Hydraulic and Electric Elevators*, Mobile, Alabama (American Technical Society) 1918; republished by Elevator World, Inc., 1995

H.D. James, "Electric Elevator Control Systems," *American Electrician*, November 1902, pp. 515–18

H.D. James, "The Electric Elevator," *American Electrician*, November 1902, pp. 515–18

H.D. James, "The Electric Elevator," *American Institute of Electrical Engineers Transactions*, vol. 30, June 29, 1915

H.D. James, "The Electric Elevator," *The Electric Club Journal*, vol. 1, no. 4, May 1904, pp. 188–97

H.D. James, "Vertical Transportation," *American Architect*, vol. 225, May 7, 1924, pp. 451–54

Lubomir Janovsky, *Elevator Mechanical Design Principles and Concepts*, Ellis Horwood Series in Vertical Transportation, London (Ellis Horwood) 1987

Jardine, Hill & Murdock, "Kent Automatic Parking Garage, New York," *American Architect*, vol. 133, June 20, 1928, p. 837

Bernard L. Johnson, ed., "Two Elevators in One Shaft," *American Builder*, vol. 50, February 1931, p. 93

Bassett Jones, "The Empire State Building," *Architectural Forum*, vol. 54, January 1931, pp. 95–99

Bassett Jones, "Ups and Downs in the Modern Building," *The Journal of the American Institute of Architects*, vol. 7, no. 7, July 1924, pp. 328–31

Marilyn E. Kaplan, "Replicating Historic Elevator Enclosures: Guaranty Building Buffalo, New York," *Preservation Tech Notes*, June 1989

Edgar Kaufmann, ed., *The Rise of an American Architecture*, London (Pall Mall Press, for the Metropolitan Museum of Art, New York) 1970

Kevin Kelly, *New Rules for the New Economy*, New York (Penguin Books) 1998

W. Sloane Kennedy, "The Vertical Railway," *Harpers New Monthly Magazine*, June–November 1882, pp. 888–94

Heino A. Klaussen, "Behind the Push Buttons in Automatic Elevators," *Control Engineering*, February 1966

Charles H. Kloman, "The Growth and Development of the Elevator Industry," *Cassiers Magazine*, vol. 32, no. 5, September 1907, pp. 389–404

Charles E. Knox, "The World's Highest Office Building," *Electrical World*, vol. 62, no. 3, July 19, 1913, pp. 125–32

Rem Koolhaas et al., *Harvard Design School Guide to Shopping*, Cologne (Taschen) 2001

Otto P. Kramer, "Annual Reports Relate a History," *Elevator World*, December 1979, pp. 32–36

Michel de l'Ormeraie and Maurice Poisson, *Elevators Through the Ages*, Chambéry, France (Gemap) 1993

Miriam Lacob, "Elevators on the Move," *Scientific American*, October 1997

Vittorio Magnago Lampugnani et al., *Vertical: Lift Escalator Paternoster: A Cultural History of Vertical Transport*, Berlin (Ernst & Sohn) 1994

Sarah B. Landau and Carl W. Condit, *Rise of the New York Skyscraper, 1865-1913*, New Haven, Connecticut (Yale University Press) 1996

Eino K. Latvala, *Evolution of Elevator Technology*, Cambridge, Massachusetts (The Winthrop Group, Inc., for the Otis Elevator Company) 1991

Miriam R. Levin, *When the Eiffel Tower Was New: French Visions of Progress at the Centennial of the Revolution*, South Hadley, Massachusetts (Mount Holyoke College Art Museum/ University of Massachusetts Press) 1989

David Lindquist, "Modern Electric Elevators and Elevator Problems," *Journal of American Society of Mechanical Engineers*, April 13, 1915

David L. Lindquist, "The Past in Retrospect," December 1931

E.T. Littell, "Club Chambers and Apartment Houses," *American Architect and Building News*, February 19, 1876, p. 59

"London's New Amusement: Up and Down the Escalator," *The Illustrated London News*, October 14, 1911, pp. 592–93

Richard D. Mandell, *Paris 1900: The Great World's Fair*, Toronto (University of Toronto Press) *c.* 1967

E. Marshall, "Elevators," *The Engineers' List*, 1906, pp. 19–22

T. Commerford Martin and Joseph Wetzler, eds., "The New Headquarters of the Postal Telegraph-Cable Company, New York City: The Sprague-Pratt Electric Elevators," *The Electrical Engineer*, vol. 17, sec. II, April 18, 1894, pp. 346–47

T. Commerford Martin and Joseph Wetzler, eds., "The Reno Inclined Elevator in a Department Store," *The Electrical Engineer*, vol. 26, July 7, 1898, pp. 1–3

James A. McHollan, "Electric and Hydraulic Elevators in Modern Buildings," *Architectural Forum*, vol. 39, October 1923, pp. 169–74

Jeffrey L. Meikle, *Twentieth-Century Limited: Industrial Design in America, 1925–39*, 2nd ed Philadelphia (Temple University Press) 2001

Louis K. Meisel, *Richard Estes: The Complete Paintings*, New York (Abrams) 1986

Joseph I. Meko, "Creating and Selling a Safe Elevator: An Illustration of the Inventive Style of Elisha Graves Otis," *Westchester Historical Society*, vol. 65, no. 4, fall 1989

D.S. Meshket, ed., *Advanced Motion Control*, Ventura, California (Intertec Communications, Inc.) 1988

Edmund Mitchell, "The Paris Exposition as a Mechanical Achievement," *Engineering Magazine*, June 19, 1900

Percival Robert Moses, "Standards of Practice in Electric Elevator Installation," *The Engineering Magazine – An Industrial Review*, December 1897, pp. 479–92

La Nature, "Movable Ramps at the Paris Exposition," *Scientific American Supplement*, no. 1297, November 10, 1900, p. 20790

La Nature, "The New Elevators of the Eiffel Tower," *Scientific American Supplement*, no. 1301, December 8, 1900, pp. 20851–52

"The New Astoria Hotel," *Architecture and Building*, February 5, 1898, pp. 51–56

"New Trend – Elevators Controlled by Electrical Brains," *Engineering News*, May 7, 1953, pp. 32–34

New York Evening Post, "Elevators in Private Houses," *Architecture and Building*, vol. 28, April 19, 1898, p. 124

New York Times, "Co-Operative Apartment-Houses," *American Architect and Building News*, February 19, 1881, p. 88

Dennis Normile, "Japan Unveils New Elevator," *Engineering News Record*, June 14, 1990

A.T. North, "The Dual Elevator Has Come," *Architectural Forum*, vol. 54, February 1931, pp. 235–56

Ray Orton, *Moving People From Street to Platform: 100 Years Underground*, Mobile, Alabama (Elevator World) 2000

Benton B. Orwing, "Builder of American, Elisha Otis," *Architecture*, March 1936

"Otis Controls Elevators Electronically," *Business Week*, June 19, 1948, pp. 58–60

Otis Elevator Company, "The Autotronic Operating Programs," Otis Elevator Company Information Bulletin, B-2061, August 4, 1950

Otis Elevator Company, "Autotronic Unlimited, Instant Elevatoring," Otis Elevator Company Unnumbered Information Bulletin, no. 1964

Otis Elevator Company, "Breakthrough on the Upside: The World Trade Center," Otis Elevator Company Talk Topic, no. 5, March 12, 1969, unpublished work

Otis Elevator Company, "Detailed Description of Double Deck Elevators," Otis Elevator Company Sales Bulletin, B-307, 1932

Otis Elevator Company, "Early Elevator Development," "The First Safe elevator," "How the Otis Company Was Organized," "The Modern Elevator," and "Hydraulic Versus Electric," *The Otis Bulletin*, November 1948

Otis Elevator Company, "Electronic Signal Control," Otis Elevator Company Sales Bulletin, B-725-SW, 1948

Otis Elevator Company, "The Escalator, Earl's Court Station, London," *The Indicator*, June 1912, vol. 5, no. 6, p. 44

Otis Elevator Company, "The First One Hundred Years," Otis Elevator Company Centennial Publication, 1953

Otis Elevator Company, "Full Collective Control," Otis Elevator Company sales folder, B-656, sales reference sheet, B-2026, 1947

Otis Elevator Company, "History of the Development of the Otis Automatic Signal Control Elevator," as told to Mr. Bebb by Mr. Lindquist, November 17, 1936

Otis Elevator Company, *The Indicator Magazine*, July 1909–June 1913

Otis Elevator Company, "Introducing the Trav-O-Lator," *The Otis Bulletin*, July–August 1955

Otis Elevator Company, "Modernization Product Knowledge," binder #1 and #2, unpublished work, 1991

Otis Elevator Company, *Moving Your Customers and What They Buy. Brief Suggestions for Increasing Business by Increasing Service*, New York, 1915, p. 11

Otis Elevator Company, "Multi-Voltage Control, Its Advantages and Operation," 1922

Otis Elevator Company, "Now It's Just Touch and Go," *The Otis Bulletin*, November–December 1952, pp. 9–12

Otis Elevator Company, "Operatorless Elevators Need Not Be Voiceless," *Engineering News Record*, vol. 155, July 7, 1955, pp. 46, 50

Otis Elevator Company, "The Origin and Development of Modern Elevator Supervisory Control Systems," Otis Elevator Company Information Bulletin, B-2051, April 1948

Otis Elevator Company, "Otis Electronic Touch button Landing Fixture," Otis Elevator Company Information Bulletin, no. 2054, 1950

Otis Elevator Company, "Otis Metropolitan Steam Safety Elevator," New York, 1872

Otis Elevator Company, "Otis Signal Control Elevators," Otis Elevator Company sales folder, B-45, August 1930

Otis Elevator Company, "Otis Signal-Control: A Study of its Basic Principles and its Field of Application," Otis Elevator Company sales folder, B-4001, February 1936

Otis Elevator Company, "Otis Unit-Multi-Voltage Control for Geared-Type Elevator Machines," Otis Elevator Company sales folder, no. 4005, January 1937

Otis Elevator Company, "Otis Unit-Multi-Voltage Control," Otis Elevator Company sales folder, B-293, October 1930

Otis Elevator Company, "Partners in Progress, The National Association of Building Owners and Managers and the Otis Elevator Company," 1957

Otis Elevator Company, "Permanent Portable for the World Trade Center," *The Otis Bulletin*, 1969

Otis Elevator Company, "Tell Me About Elevators," Library of Congress catalog card no. 76-375205, 6th edn 1982

Otis Elevator Company, "War Production at Otis," *United-News Journal*, Hartford, Connecticut (United Technologies Corporation) November/December 1989, p. 2

"Paris Universal Exposition, 1900," *Manufacturer and Builder*, vol. 26, no. 8, August 1900

Ferdinand W. Peck, "The United States at the Paris Exposition in 1900," *The North American Review*, vol. 168, no. 506, January 1899

Tom F. Peters, *Building the Nineteenth Century*, Cambridge, Massachusetts (MIT Press) 1996

L.A. Petersen, "Elisha Graves Otis 1811–1861, and His Influence Upon Vertical Transportation", *The Newcomen Society of England American Branch*, 1945

Antoine Picon, *L'Art de l'ingenieur: constructeur, entrepreneur, inventeur*, Paris (Le Moniteur) 1997

Kenneth Powell, *New London Architecture*, London (Merrell) 2001

Charles R. Pratt, "Elevators," *American Society of Mechanical Engineering Transactions*, vol. 20, 1899, pp. 805–72

Thomas B. Preston, "A Reading Journey Through France," *The Chatauquan*, vol. 6, no. 30, pp. 616–28

Cedric Price, *Cedric Price, Architectural Association Works*, II, London (Architectural Association) 1984

Louis M. Ralston, "The Engineer's Problem in Tall Buildings," *Architectural Forum*, vol. 52, June 1930, pp. 909–11

Jan Seidler Ramirez et al., *Painting the Town: Cityscapes of New York from the Museum of the City of New York*, New Haven, Connecticut (Yale University Press) 2000

Harrison P. Reed, "Electric Power Application to Passenger and Freight Elevators," *A.I.E.E. Journal*, January–February 1922, pp. 57–67, 142–64

J.W. Reno, "The Reno Continuous Passenger Elevator," *Engineering News*, August 25, 1892, pp. 188–89

"The Reno Inclined Elevator," *Scientific American*, January 16, 1897, p. 41

P. Riani and P. Goldberger, *The Skyscraper*, New York (Knopf) 1980

P. Riani, P. Goldberger, and J. Portman, *John Portman*, Milan (L'Arcaedizioni) 1990

Brian Richards, *Moving in Cities*, Boulder, Colorado (Westview Press) 1976

Brian Richards, *New Movement in Cities*, London (Studio Vista) 1966

S.P. Ring, "The Escalator for Department Stores," *Architects' and Builders' Magazine*, vol. 44, December 1912, pp. 509–14

Patrick Rogers, "Vertical Leap," *Preservation Magazine*, May/June 1998

"The Rolling Platform at the Exposition of 1900," *Scientific American Supplement*, no. 1279, July 7, 1900, pp. 20504-05

Joseph Sachs, "Electric Elevators," *Cassiers Magazine*, part II, April 10, 1897, pp. 475–76

Joseph Sachs, "Electric Elevators," *Cassiers Magazine*, part III, April 17, 1897, pp. 506–07

Joseph Sachs, "Electric Elevators," *Cassiers Magazine*, part IV, April 24, 1897, pp. 530–34

Joseph Sachs, "Electric Elevators," *Cassiers Magazine*, part V, May 1, 1897, pp. 557–83

Joseph Sachs, "Electric Elevators," *Cassiers Magazine*, part VI, May 8, 1897, pp. 581–83

Joseph Sachs, "Electric Elevators," *Cassiers Magazine*, part VII, May 22, 1897, pp. 643–46

Joseph Sachs, "Electric Elevators," *Cassiers Magazine*, part VIII, no. 4, August 1895, pp. 387–408

John Salustri, "Upwardly Mobile," *Better Buildings*, October 1991

Joris Schroeder, "Elevator Traction Drives – A Review of the Present State of the Art," *Elevator World*, May 1988

"See Height Limit Reached," *New York Times*, April 13, 1931

Charles D. Seeberger, "The Escalator," *Cassier's Engineering Monthly*, March 1904, p. 458

Allan Sekula, *Fish Story*, Düsseldorf (Richter Verlag) 1995

James W. Shepp and Daniel B. Shepp, *Shepp's World's Fair Photographed, 1893, Being a Collection of Original Copyrighted Photographs*, Chicago (Globe Bible Publishing Co.) 1893

Robert M. Sheridan, "The Evolution of the Elevator," *Association of Engineering Societies Transactions*, May 1880, pp. 584–88

R.H. Shreve, "The Economic Design of Office Buildings," *Architectural Record*, vol. 67, 1930, pp. 354–59

"The Singer Building, New York," *Architects' and Builders' Magazine*, July 1908, pp. 429–45

"Speeding Up the Elevator for Our Taller Buildings," *New York Times* (Science Section) April 5, 1931, pp. 4–6

Theodore Stanton, "The International Exhibition of 1900," *The Century Magazine*, vol. 51, no. 2, New York (The Century Company) December 1895

William T. Stead, "The Paris Exposition," *The Cosmopolitan*, August 1900, pp. 339–60

"Steam Versus Stairs: the Movable Room in the Fifth Avenue Hotel," *New York Times*, January 23, 1860

Robert A.M. Stern, Thomas Mellins and David Fishman, *New York 1880: Architecture and Urbanism in the Gilded Age*, New York (Monacelli Press) 1999

Robert A.M. Stern, Thomas Mellins and David Fishman, *New York 1960: Architecture and Urbanism Between the Second World War and the Bicentennial*, New York (Monacelli Press) 1995

Jean Stienmann, *Pascal*, New York (Harcourt, Brace & World) 1966

James Stirling, Michael Wilford and Associates, Buildings and Projects 1975–1992, Stuttgart (Verlag Gerd Hatje) 1994

George R. Strakosch, "Modernization of the Flatiron Building Classical Update," *Elevator World*, October 1999

George R. Strakosch, ed., *The Vertical Transportation Handbook*, 3rd edn New York (John Wiley & Sons) 1998

Robert L. Streeter, "Handling Materials in Manufacturing Plants, Section V, Vertical Elevators, Inclined Elevators," *The Engineering Magazine*, vol. 50, March 1916, pp. 869–96

Deyan Sudjic, *New Directions in British Architecture: Norman Foster, Richard Rogers, James Stirling*, London (Thames and Hudson) 1986

Henry Harrison Suplee, "Local Transportation at the Paris Exposition," *Engineering Magazine*, August 19, 1900

Allan Temko, "Theatrics Packing Them In at San Francisco Centre," *San Francisco Chronicle*, November 14, 1988

Michael Topel, "Ancient Escalator Was a Link to History," *The Patriot-Ledger*, April 3, 1995

Josephine Tozier, "National Pavilions at the Paris Exposition," *Overland Monthly and Out West Magazine*, vol. 35, no. 209, May 1900

"Traveling Stairways for the Elevated Railways, New York," *Scientific American*, November 17, 1900, p. 313

"Up and Down, Electronically," *Business Week*, November 20, 1949, pp. 50–52

Alexander Verbraeck and Corné Versteegt, "Logistical Control for Fully Automated Large-Scale Freight Transport Systems," Delft University of Technology, 2000

C. Versteegt and H.G. Sol, "The Design of Logistic Control for Intermodal Transport Chains of the 21st Century," TRAIL Research School, Delft University of Technology, December, 1999, p. 14

"Vertical Transport Systems Get TLC at WTC," *Buildings, The Construction and Building Management Journal*, 1969

Robert M. Vogel, "Elevator Systems of the Eiffel Tower, 1889," *Contributions from The Museum of History and Technology*, paper 19, Washington, D.C. (Smithsonian Institution Press) 1961

Robert M. Vogel, *A Museum Case Study: The Acquisition of a Small Residential Elevator*, Washington D.C. (Smithsonian Institution Press) 1988

Michael Wagner, "Making it to the Top," *Architecture*, May 1990, pp. 86–89

Henry C. Walker, "Reminiscences of 70 Years in the Lift Industry," Gloucester, UK (John Bellows) 1934

Colson Whitehead, *The Intuitionist*, New York (Anchor Books) 1999

Richard Guy Wilson, "Transportation Machine Design," *The Machine Age in America, 1918–1941*, New York (Brooklyn Museum of Art/Harry Abrams) 1986

William Worthington, Jr., "Early Risers," *Invention and Technology*, winter 1989

Julie Wosk, *Breaking Frame: Technology and the Visual Arts in the Nineteenth Century*, New Brunswick, New Jersey (Rutgers University Press) 1992

Julie Wosk, *Women and the Machine: Representations From the Spinning Wheel to the Electronic Age*, Baltimore (Johns Hopkins University Press) 2001

E.W. Yearsley, "The Development of the Elevator," February 11, 1932

E.W. Yearsley, "Forty-Three Stories of Vertical Traffic (New Yorker Hotel)" *Power*, November 26, 1929

E.W. Yearsley, "Good Elevator Service for Office Buildings," Otis Elevator Company Sales Folder, B-299, March 1932

E.W. Yearsley, *Electrical Elevators*, Erskine Engineering Series for Power Plant Engineers, Executives and Students, ed. Harry E. Erskine, Boston, 1932

John Zukowsky and Martha Thorne, *Skyscrapers: The New Millennium*, Munich (The Art Institute of Chicago/ Prestel) 2000

Photography Credits

Cameron Menzies, adapted from the novel *The Shape of Things to Come* by H.G. Wells, London Film Productions, 1936; **090**: Copyright © Bettmann / CORBIS; **091**: Courtesy Museum of History and Industry, Seattle; **092**: Courtesy Photograph Collection, San Diego Historical Society; **093**: Courtesy Museum of History and Industry, Seattle; **094**: Copyright © John Portman & Associates. Courtesy John Portman & Associates; **095–097**: Timothy Hursley. Courtesy John Portman & Associates; **098**: Courtesy Phil Patton; **099**: Courtesy Todd Eberle. Originally published in *Vanity Fair*; **100**: Margaret Bourke-White / TimePix. Courtesy Harry Ransom Humanities Research Center, The University of Texas at Austin; **101**: General Motors Corporation. Used with permission, GM Media Archive; **102**: Courtesy MK Automation Engineering, Inc.; **103**: W. Huthmacher. Courtesy Elevator World, Inc.; **104**: Paul Bailey. Courtesy Advanced Transport Systems Ltd., www.alsltd.co.uk; **105**: Courtesy Maersk, Inc.; **106**: Courtesy Bernd Dahlmann; **107**: Courtesy Bernd Dahlmann; **108**: Courtesy Wildeck, Inc.; **109**: Courtesy FROG Navigation Systems; **110**: Nick Souza. Courtesy Maersk, Inc.; **111**: Courtesy of Hong Kong Air Cargo Terminals Limited; **112**: Courtesy Hong Kong Air Cargo Terminals Limited; **113**: Courtesy FROG Navigation Systems; **114**: Courtesy the Port of Long Beach; **115**: Courtesy FROG Navigation Systems; **116**: Courtesy Schindler Elevator Corporation; **117**: Courtesy of Swisslog; **118**: Copyright © Kelvin Fields. Courtesy SkyscraperPage.com; **119**: Drawing by Richard Evans. Adapted from William Marlin, "Sears Tower," *Architectural Forum*, Vol. 140, January–February 1974, pp. 12–15; "Elevator System for World's Tallest," *Elevator World*, August 1972; "Project of the Year Category 2 Elevator Modernization: Sears Tower Observation Cars Modernization," *The Elevator World Source 2001–2002*, Mobile, Alabama (Elevator World, Inc.) 2001, pp. 406–08; and "Mega-High-Rise Elevatoring" by James W. Fortune, *Elevator World*, December 1997, pp. 128–135. Courtesy National Building Museum, Washington, D.C.; **120**: Courtesy Swisslog; **121**: Courtesy Hillwood Development Corporation; **122**: Courtesy Otis Historical Archives; **123**: Courtesy Otis Historical Archives; **124**: Courtesy Museum of the City of New York, Gift of Otto Roethlisberger; **125**: Courtesy Museum of the City of New York; **126**: Courtesy Otis Historical Archives; **127**: Courtesy Otis Historical Archives; **128**: From *Scientific American*, January 16, 1897, p. 41. Courtesy Library of Congress, Washington, D.C.; **129**: Courtesy Otis Historical Archives; **130**: Courtesy Library of Congress, Washington, D.C.; **131**: Courtesy Otis Historical Archives; **132**: Courtesy Otis Historical Archives; **133**: Courtesy Library of Congress, Washington, D.C.; **134**: Courtesy Otis Historical Archives; **135**: Courtesy Julie Wosk; **136–141**: Courtesy Otis Historical Archives; **142**: Courtesy Office of War Information, Prints & Photographs Division, Library of Congress, Washington, D.C.; **143**: Museum of the City of New York, Gift of the Artist; **144**: Private collection; **145**: From *Elevator World*, 1997, pp. 56–57. Courtesy Elevator World, Inc.; **146**: From *Elevator World*, 1997, pp. 38–39. Used with permission of Schindler Elevator Corporation. Courtesy Elevator World, Inc.; **147**: Courtesy Otis Historical Archives; **148**: Courtesy Mitsubishi Electric Corporation; **149**: Copyright © Steve McCurry / Magnum Photos; **150**: Courtesy Stephan Braunfels Architekten; **151–154**: Courtesy of Universal Studios Licensing LLLP; **155**: Reprinted with permission of John Wiley & Sons, Inc.; **156**: Copyright © Nouvelles Editions de Films. Courtesy Nouvelles Editions des Films and Manuel Malle; **157–180**: Film by Thomas Edison; Courtesy Motion Picture, Broadcasting and Recorded Sound Division, Library of Congress, Washington, D.C.; **181–204**: Film by Thomas Edison; Courtesy Motion Picture, Broadcasting and Recorded Sound Division, Library of Congress, Washington, D.C.; **205**: Courtesy Warner Brothers; **206**: Courtesy of MGM CLIP + STILL; **207**: Courtesy Jerry Ohlinger's Movie Material Store, Inc.; **208**: Courtesy of Universal Studios Licensing LLLP; **209**: Courtesy Jerry Ohlinger's Movie Material Store, Inc.; **210**: Courtesy Otis Historical Archives; **211**: Courtesy Cabinet of American Illustration, Prints & Photographs Division, Library of Congress, Washington, D.C.; **212**: Courtesy Cabinet of American Illustration, Prints & Photographs Division, Library of Congress, Washington, D.C.; **213**: Courtesy Paramount Pictures; **214**: Jack Delano. Courtesy Office of War Information, Prints & Photographs Division, Library of Congress, Washington, D.C.;

p. 196: Courtesy Otis Elevator Company; **p. 197 top**: Used with permission of Elevator World, Inc; **p. 197 bottom**: Courtesy Otis Historical Archives; **p. 198**: Courtesy Otis Elevator Company; **p. 199 top**: Used with permission of Matot, Inc.; **p. 199 bottom**: Used with permission of Elevator World, Inc.; **p. 200**: Courtesy Otis Elevator Company; **p. 201 top**: Used with permission of Elevator World, Inc.; **p. 201 bottom**: Courtesy Otis Historical Archives; **p. 202**: Copyright © 1999 Elevator World, Inc. Courtesy Elevator World, Inc.; **p. 203**: Copyright © 1999 Elevator World, Inc. Courtesy Elevator World, Inc.; **p. 204**: Copyright © 1999 Elevator World, Inc. Courtesy Elevator World, Inc.; **p. 205**: Copyright © 1999 Elevator World, Inc. Courtesy Elevator World, Inc.;

Index